NONVIOLENCE
AND
SOCIAL
MOVEMENTS

The Teachings of Rev. James M. Lawson Jr.

Edited by

Kent Wong, Ana Luz González, and
Rev. James M. Lawson Jr.

UCLA Center for Labor Research and Education

Los Angeles, California

Cover photo courtesy of UCLA Labor Center
Book design by Wendell Pascual

UCLA Center for Labor Research and Education
Los Angeles, CA 90095-1478
© 2016 by UCLA Center for Labor Research and Education
All rights reserved. Published 2016
Printed in the United States of America

Library of Congress Control Number: 2015941644
ISBN: 978-0-9836289-6-5

This book is dedicated to the multitude of people, unnamed and unheralded, **who have embraced nonviolence in the struggle for equality**, liberty, and justice for all, and who continue to **fill the world with peace and hope**.

Rev. James M. Lawson Jr., March 1, 1960. *Photograph by Paul Schleicher for the* Nashville Banner. *Courtesy of the Nashville Public Library, Special Collections.*

CONTENTS

PREFACE
Kent Wong

vii

ACKNOWLEDGMENTS

ix

INTRODUCTION: TEACHING NONVIOLENCE
Kent Wong and Ana Luz González

1

THE PHILOSOPHY OF NONVIOLENCE
Preeti Sharma

5

AWAKENING: THE MONTGOMERY BUS BOYCOTT
Caroline Luce

29

THE NASHVILLE SIT-INS: A MODEL FOR A MOVEMENT
Caitlin Parker

51

THE GRAPE BOYCOTT
Preeti Sharma, Mayra Jones, and Sophia Cheng

71

HOTEL WORKERS TRANSFORM THE LABOR MOVEMENT
Caitlin Parker

87

UNDOCUMENTED AND UNAFRAID: THE IMMIGRANT YOUTH MOVEMENT
Alma Mirell Castrejon

105

BIBLIOGRAPHY

127

CONTRIBUTORS

135

Rev. James M. Lawson Jr. with his wife, Dorothy Wood Lawson, and his son John C. Lawson II, Memphis, 1969.
Courtesy of Rev. James M. Lawson Jr.

PREFACE

THE MAN AND THE MOVEMENT

Rev. James M. Lawson Jr. has been a powerful force for nonviolence and social change for many decades. One of the highlights of my career has been the privilege of working with Rev. Lawson for more than thirty years.

Rev. Lawson was a leader of the Nashville sit-in movement, which challenged Jim Crow and inspired and mobilized a new generation of young leaders who led sit-ins, marches, and freedom rides, and who changed the course of US history. He was a leader of the Memphis sanitation worker strike, which forged unprecedented alliances between the civil rights movement and the labor movement; it advanced the slogan I Am A Man in an environment where African American men were being denied basic respect and dignity.

Since coming to Los Angeles in 1974, where he served as pastor for Holman United Methodist Church until his retirement in 1999, Rev. Lawson has emerged as an energizing force for nonviolent social change, for peace, and for justice. When I was a staff attorney at the Service Employees International Union in the 1980s, Rev. Lawson convened a small group of us at the church. We called ourselves the "Holman Group." We were a ragtag group of inexperienced organizers like Antonio Villaraigosa (long before he became mayor of Los Angeles), Maria Elena Durazo (long before she led the Los Angeles labor movement), Gilbert Cedillo (long before he became a member of the California state legislature and the LA city council), Karen Bass (long before she became a member of Congress), along with other upstarts who wanted to change the world. Rev. Lawson taught us about the power of nonviolence, about the necessity of strategy and tactics, about the importance of reflection and planning, and about how we must prepare ourselves for a lifetime of work for justice. Rev. Lawson taught us about "plantation capitalism." He taught us that there are no short cuts to building a social justice movement, and that in the majority of campaigns—in the majority of battles that we wage—we may not win. But that we must persevere and move forward, for in the words of his good friend Dr. Martin Luther King Jr., "The arc of the moral universe is long, but it bends towards justice."

During the campaign to transform the Los Angeles labor movement, Rev. Lawson was on the front lines, preparing the hotel workers for civil disobedience as they fought some of the most powerful hotel corporations in the world. He taught the workers as they were getting arrested to engage the police in conversation, to explain what they were doing, and to maintain the moral high ground.

During a Justice for Janitors campaign, I remember being part of a building take-over with hundreds of Latino immigrant janitors. There, seated in the corner, was Rev. Lawson, providing spiritual guidance and wisdom. The immigrant janitors may not have spoken the same language, but they understood the power of his words and his actions.

When the home care workers of Los Angeles began to organize, many were convinced they had no chance of winning. How could a group of low-wage women of color, in separate homes and in scattered neighborhoods, ever succeed in building a union? But Rev. Lawson was there on the first picket lines, encouraging them to move forward. And he was there when 74,000 home care workers celebrated their victory, which was the largest union organizing campaign in the country in decades.

In 2006, during the largest May Day demonstration in US history, I had the privilege of marching four miles down Wilshire Boulevard with Rev. Lawson. Block after block, mile after mile, I asked Rev. Lawson if he wanted to rest or if I should arrange for transportation for the rest of the journey. Rev. Lawson declined. He marched every step of the way, and at the end, he jumped up on stage to give a powerful speech defending immigrant rights, declaring, "No human being is illegal."

When we launched Dream Summer, the first national internship program for undocumented immigrant students, Rev. Lawson was there. He came to listen to our students, to hear their stories, and to encourage them to keep going. And they learned from Rev. Lawson. They launched hunger strikes and sit-ins and courageous civil disobedience actions, risking arrest and deportation. In 2012 they won a historic victory when the Obama administration agreed to stop the deportation of undocumented immigrant youth and to grant them the opportunity to apply for work authorization.

Rev. Lawson is a man of humility, of compassion, of justice. When you have the opportunity to work with Rev. Lawson, to watch him interact with others, to learn from him, you cannot help but become a better person yourself. I will forever be grateful that he has been a part of my life. I will forever be grateful for his guidance and leadership, for his friendship and mentorship, and for teaching me the power of nonviolence.

Kent Wong
Director, UCLA Center for Labor Research and Education
March 2016

ACKNOWLEDGMENTS

The editors thank the César E. Chávez Department of Chicana/o Studies, the African American Studies Center, the UCLA Office of Instructional Development, and the Institute for Research on Labor and Employment at UCLA for their generous support for this project. We also are grateful to Rebecca Frazier for her excellent copyediting and Wendell Pascual for the cover and overall design of the book.

We met on several occasions at the UCLA Center for Labor Research and Education and the Downtown Labor Center for this project, and we thank the staffs at both these organizations for their extensive support of this project. Julie Monroe, Elizabeth Espinoza, Andrea Arias, Claudia Suarez, and Natalia Garcia were especially helpful.

Thanks also to Gabriela Rios, Diana Valenzuela, and Samantha Blanco, who meticulously transcribed Rev. Lawson's class lectures and his subsequent conversations with chapter authors. Will Wiltschko and Maria Duque were instrumental in securing some of the photographs and illustrations in this publication. Finally, special thanks to the UCLA students that participated in the 2013 spring graduate seminar and helped with earlier drafts during the initial stage in developing the chapters for this publication: Jason Ball, Sophia Cheng, Regem Corpuz, Jonathan Freeman, Alexis Gardner, Mayra Jones, Hyacinth Noble, Jennifer Regas, Kendy Rivera, Silvia Rodriguez, Carlos Rogel, Rachel Sanoff, Leslie Serrano, Rachel Shuen, Angela Tea, Tracy Teel, and Will Wiltschko. We also benefited immensely from the assistance of Kelly Lytle Hernandez, who helped to teach the graduate seminar and provided advice and input with earlier manuscripts.

We would also like to thank the guest speakers who participated in the graduate seminar and who inspired our students in their research, including civil rights veteran Bernard Lafayette, UFW co-founder Dolores Huerta, Los Angeles labor leader Maria Elena Durazo, and immigrant youth leaders Neidi Dominguez, Sofia Campos, and Carlos Amador. They represent an amazing group of individuals who have applied the philosophy of nonviolence to US social movements and have witnessed its transformative power through their own lives and work. We celebrate their contributions, and all nonviolent activists who have advanced historic movements for social and economic justice.

Kent Wong
Director, UCLA Center for Labor Research and Education

Ana Luz González
Project Coordinator, UC Irvine Community and Labor Project

Rev. James M. Lawson Jr., Dolores Huerta, and Kent Wong at a graduate seminar at the University of California, Los Angeles, on May 8, 2013. *Courtesy of Pocho Sanchez.*

TEACHING NONVIOLENCE

Kent Wong and Ana Luz González

For over a decade Rev. James M. Lawson Jr. has taught a course sponsored by the UCLA Labor Center titled "Nonviolence and Social Movements." It has been one of the most popular classes at UCLA, especially among student leaders and activists. Hundreds of students have been inspired by Lawson to engage in the study of nonviolence and to explore its application to contemporary social movements within the United States and internationally. Many of these young people have gone on to become leaders in their own right who have dedicated their lives to social justice. The course has also attracted hotel workers, janitors, home care workers, and campus service workers.

Lawson's course traces the development of nonviolence, which is rooted in the philosophy and practices of Mohandas Gandhi, and draws on Lawson's own experiences as a young man studying and working in India. The course examines powerful nonviolent campaigns led by Lawson, beginning in 1960 with the Nashville sit-in movement, which helped to desegregate lunch counters during the early years of the civil rights movement. Lawson also teaches students about the Memphis sanitation workers strike in 1968, which successfully organized African American workers in the South, and he relates how his good friend Dr. Martin Luther King Jr. joined the effort in Memphis, Tennessee. King, an advocate for nonviolence, was assassinated while organizing with the sanitation workers.

The curriculum examines other historic US social movements that have effectively embraced the philosophy of nonviolence, beginning in the 1910s with the women's suffrage campaign. The US labor movement is also emphasized in the class, from the use of non-violence in the sit-down strikes in Detroit in the 1930s that led to the birth of industrial unionism to the organizing of farmworkers led by César Chávez and Dolores Huerta in the 1960s. The course also addresses the nonviolent strategy and tactics recently employed by courageous undocumented youth who have risked arrest and deportation in their fight for immigrant rights.

Lawson's curriculum also covers international experiences in nonviolence, from the historic workers' movement in the Gdansk shipyards of Poland, which toppled a totalitarian government in 1981, to the anti-apartheid campaign in South Africa, which succeeded in overthrowing the repressive white minority regime in 1992.

Despite the deep historical importance of nonviolent movements, few publications have captured their stories, particularly from the perspective of leaders and activists who have thoughtfully applied the philosophy of nonviolence in their campaigns. We at the UCLA Labor Center were enthusiastic about developing a publication that could present Lawson's teachings on nonviolence, his reflections on more than sixty years of the theory and practice of nonviolence, and how those teachings have been embraced by social justice movements at local, state, national, and global levels.

In Spring 2013 the UCLA Labor Center offered a graduate seminar that was designed to encourage student research into key US nonviolent movements and to provide a foundation for this publication. The syllabus was built around Lawson's reflections on the philosophy of nonviolence, and class sessions provided a setting for thoughtful conversations between Lawson and other nationally recognized leaders who are committed to nonviolence, including civil rights veteran Bernard Layette and United Farm Workers co-founder Dolores Huerta. Los Angeles labor leader Maria Elena Durazo, who led Hotel Employees and Restaurant Employees (HERE) Local 11, also participated as a guest in the class; she discussed Lawson's role as her mentor during the transformation of Local 11 and its creative use of nonviolence. Finally, one class featured a panel of immigrant youth leaders who engaged in a dialogue with Lawson about the application of nonviolence in their campaign for passage of the DREAM Act and their demand that the Obama administration stop the deportation of immigrant youth.

This publication is the culmination of a two-year collaboration with Lawson and the chapter authors to document the historic contributions of Lawson and to assess the philosophy of nonviolence in the context of social change movements today. It provided an opportunity for the young scholars in the graduate seminar to reflect and write on the use of nonviolence to advance social justice causes. It is the first book to synthesize Lawson's reflections on nonviolence and the first to examine five critical nonviolent movements of the past sixty years that have helped to transform US society.

Lawson guided this process from beginning to end. He meticulously read every page numerous times to make sure that the texts accurately capture the philosophy of nonviolence and its impact on powerful social movements. His intent is to provide an important learning resource for students of nonviolence and social movements, one that links theory with practice and analysis with action. Lawson believes that this pedagogical methodology fulfills the central mission of the public university: to encourage critical thinking, to promote research that is grounded in people's experience, and to inspire public service.

The first chapter, on the philosophy of nonviolence, draws heavily from Lawson's teachings and lectures. Lawson has taught nonviolence nationally and internationally, and for decades he has been called upon to advise social justice leaders on the theory and practice of nonviolence. Although one chapter could never fully capture the creative and diverse nonviolence curriculum that Lawson has developed and modified over the years, this introductory chapter synthesizes the major tenets of nonviolence and serves to encourage other scholars and activists to pursue the research of nonviolence in more detail.

Following the first chapter are five case studies that reflect the use of nonviolence within powerful social movements in the United States. The first three chapters explore well-known examples of nonviolent campaigns. The Montgomery bus boycott in 1955, the first mass nonviolent campaign, helped launch the civil rights movement and brought international attention to King and to Rosa Parks. The Nashville sit-in campaign in 1960 was led directly by Lawson. It not only helped to desegregate lunch counters in Nashville and throughout the South but also provided opportunities to recruit and train a new generation of young leaders. These young activists went on to build a powerful civil rights movement in the South. The third chapter highlights the grape boycott, which galvanized millions of people across the globe to support the organizing efforts of the United Farm Workers, led by Chávez and Huerta. The fourth chapter captures the breakthrough work of HERE Local 11, which served as a catalyst for the transformation of the Los Angeles and, indeed, the national labor movement. The final chapter captures one of the most powerful youth movements in recent decades, in which undocumented immigrant students implemented nonviolent strategies and tactics to launch and win campaigns for civil and human rights.

Lawson has emerged as one of the most powerful and eloquent advocates for nonviolence in the history of the United States. His teachings have been embraced by organizers and activists who have had the privilege of working with him in Tennessee and California, but his influence has spread throughout the country and across the globe. This publication first and foremost is a tribute to this courageous visionary. Yet the impact of Lawson's teachings reaches far beyond any individual contribution to social change. Lawson's teachings have been integrated into a broad array of social justice movements worldwide.

Lawson has been a teacher of nonviolence for more than six decades, so it is fitting that this publication has emerged from a class on nonviolence that he taught. And although he generously shares his profound and insightful reflections on nonviolence, in this book he chose to focus on how nonviolence has been used as a powerful force for change in campaigns throughout the United States. These campaigns were led by ordinary people who, through the effective use of nonviolence, accomplished extraordinary things. This is the power of Lawson's teachings. This is the power of nonviolence.

We sincerely hope that this publication will inspire, challenge, and motivate a new generation of social change agents to carry on the work of those who have gone before us.

Participants in the "Nonviolence and Social Movements" class, May 8, 2013. Second row (left to right): Pocho Sanchez, Carlos Rogel, Caitlin Parker, Tracy Teel, Will Wiltschko, Kelly Lytle Hernandez, Jonathan Freeman, Ana Luz González, and Kent Wong. First row (left to right): Leslie Serrano, Rev. James M. Lawson Jr., Dolores Huerta, Preeti Sharma, Mayra Jones, Rachel Shuen, Sophia Cheng, and Angela Tea. *Courtesy of Pocho Sanchez.*

Rev. James M. Lawson Jr., Rev. Martin Luther King Jr., and Rev. H. Ralph Jackson speak in support of striking sanitation workers at a press conference in Memphis on March 28, 1968. *Courtesy of Preservation and Special Collections, University Libraries, University of Memphis.*

CHAPTER 1

THE PHILOSOPHY OF NONVIOLENCE

Preeti Sharma

I have been convinced for nearly twelve years now that the only hope for the Negro in this country is a genuine movement of nonviolence which reflects many of the characteristics of the Montgomery boycott and which strikes not only at the fear of the Negro but also at the power structure of the nation which continues to perpetuate social injustice. If this is to happen it will be because of the ministry uniting as one body and giving initiative [and] leadership to the countless number of Negroes who urgently want such leadership.
—Letter from James M. Lawson Jr. to Martin Luther King Jr., November 3, 1958

On February 6, 1957, two young black ministers shook hands in Ohio for the first time. One of the young men was Martin Luther King Jr. The leader of the successful Montgomery bus boycott, which had ended less than two months before, King had surfaced as a major figure in the growing desegregation movement.[1] His picture could be found on the front pages of newspapers across the United States and around the globe. The other minister, James M. Lawson Jr., was a scholar and an emerging activist who had returned from one year of incarceration in a federal penitentiary for resisting the draft. He had spent the next three years in India, where he had worked as a campus minister, physical education teacher, and coach. Lawson was a student and practitioner of Mohandas Gandhi's philosophy of nonviolence as well as a scholar of the Bible. The two men had never met before that day in 1957, although Lawson had read much about King. King, who recognized the depth of Lawson's knowledge of nonviolence, encouraged Lawson to move to the South immediately, saying, "We need you right now."[2]

Lawson, like King, believes in the power of nonviolence as a theory, a philosophy, and a methodology to challenge unjust laws and policies and to advance community needs, job access, and dignity for all Americans.[3] Nonviolence has the power to eradicate structural racism, sexism, and violence and to emancipate working people. Lawson has extended his expertise in nonviolence to a number of movements over the past five decades, offering workshops and consultations. He has been a pioneer, helping initiate nonviolent marches, boycotts, and direct action campaigns that have changed the lives of millions. The night before he was assassinated, King called Lawson "the leading theorist and strategist of nonviolence in the world."[4] This chapter will document Lawson's lifelong pursuit of social justice through nonviolence.

A SHORT BIOGRAPHY

James Morris Lawson Jr. was born on September 22, 1928, in Uniontown, Pennsylvania, and was raised in Massillon, Ohio. He was the eighth of twelve children in an immigrant family deeply rooted in the church. His paternal great-grandfather and grandfather, both named Henry Dangerfield Lawson Jr., had escaped slavery in the South and made a harrowing journey to Canada. They became farmers in Guelph, Ontario. His grandfather was also a pastor. His father, James Morris Lawson Sr., a Methodist minister, left Canada and immigrated to the United States. Lawson's mother, Philane Mae Cover, also a dedicated Christian, had emigrated from Jamaica and raised her children while working at home as a seamstress. Lawson recalled how Christianity influenced him as a young child: "My parentage and my family in this religious background made me sense at a fairly early age that I belonged, that I was a human being."[5] Despite this sense of acceptance, as he grew up in Ohio he experienced the humiliating and dehumanizing effects of racism and prejudice.[6] His father always insisted that he stay strong and defend himself, while his mother taught him that the mistreatment of other people was not allowed in Jesus's teachings.

He was four years old when he experienced racism and physical violence for the first time. As he was playing in a local park in Massillon, a child addressed him with a racial epithet, and Lawson hit him. The most memorable incident happened in the fourth grade, while Lawson was running an errand for his family. A white child in a parked car yelled the "N-word" at him, and Lawson slapped the child in response. Lawson returned home and reported the incident to his mother. She calmly asked him, "Jimmie, what good did that do?" She then reaffirmed him as a person in a long soliloquy that ended with, "There must be a better way." Lawson related that this moment was "a numinous experience, defined by mystics and theologians . . . as when the world stands still and you hear voices, but most of all you make decisions." "At that age," Lawson reflected, "I said to myself, 'Never again will I use my fists on the playground when I get angry or when someone else gets angry with me.' And I heard myself saying, 'I do not know what the better way is, but I will find it.'"[7] Lawson had begun his search for a better way to cope with racial hostility, a pursuit that unfolded in the decades to come.

Lawson experienced racial violence on a personal level as a child, but as he grew older he also developed an awareness of structural violence. "By the time I was in high school," he recalled, "I recognized that all the elements of racism and bigotry were wrong and that I would not imitate any of that to the best of my ability. As I read about segregation and racism in the country, I recognized that those laws I would not obey."[8] Noting the pervasiveness of segregation and racism, Lawson pursued a path of justice that challenged those attitudes and laws. He conducted his first sit-in when he was a junior in high school. While attending a youth conference in Indianapolis, he remained at the counter of Long's Drugstore for over an hour when he was refused service.[9]

It was while he was in high school that Lawson determined that he would follow his calling and become a pastor, like his father and paternal grandfather. He received his high school diploma in 1946, and in 1947 he began studying at Baldwin-Wallace College, a Methodist school in Berea, Ohio. During his first year at Baldwin-Wallace, Lawson met two influential civil rights leaders, A. G. Muste and Bayard Rustin.[10]

James Morris Lawson Sr. (Lawson's father) and Philane Mae Cover (Lawson's mother) in Memphis. Rev. James M. Lawson Jr.'s high school photograph. *Courtesy of Rev. James M. Lawson Jr.*

Muste, the head of the Fellowship of Reconciliation (FOR), an international pacifist organization, had been invited by the college's history department to present a series of lectures in the fall of 1947. His talk on Gandhi was particularly significant for the young scholar. Muste's comments, and the subsequent conversation that the two men had over dinner, inspired Lawson to read everything he could on Christian pacifism. Lawson recalled that among these works was Gandhi's *"The Story of My Experiments with Truth*, which is the autobiography, [and] some of his speeches."[11] Gandhi's thoughts on nonviolence spoke to Lawson, presenting a method for fighting and resisting racism, segregation, and economic injustice while stressing the futility of violence. Following their meeting at Baldwin-Wallace, Muste and Lawson continued to have serious conversations over the following years on nonviolent action and the writings of Gandhi.[12]

Lawson met Rustin in 1948 at a statewide Methodist student conference in Ohio. Rustin, who was active in FOR and the Congress for Racial Equality (CORE), had been arrested in 1947 for his participation in the first of the Freedom Rides, called the "Journey of Reconciliation."[13] During this formative period, Lawson also deepened his biblical studies. Jesus's stories of resistance helped formulate his views on unconditional love, and Lawson drew parallels between Jesus's and Gandhi's teachings on love and social justice. Lawson joined the FOR, whose principles influenced his thoughts on peace and racial justice. In 1948, two years before the outbreak of the Korean War, military conscription was reinstated with the passage of the Selective Service Act. Lawson, a Christian African American man living in a racially discriminatory country, was faced with

Nonviolence is love in action. And love, as Gandhi understood it, is the call that creation tells us to **respect all of life**. And to even have confidence in life. So, he calls love . . . trust in life, **respect for life, reverence for life**.

—Rev. Lawson April 2013

an ethical problem. Although he had registered when he turned eighteen, Lawson believed that the draft was antithetical to his faith and his sense of justice. He concluded that the draft was immoral, as was Jim Crow.[14] "I called myself, by the time I was a sophomore or junior in college, a draft resistor," Lawson remembers. "I sent my draft cards back."[15] In the fall of 1950, in his senior year in college, he was arrested. He was tried in April 1951 and sentenced to three years in prison.[16]

Lawson was incarcerated at a federal work camp in Mill Point, West Virginia. The minimum-security facility primarily held conscientious objectors and moonshiners. Although living quarters were segregated, African American and white prisoners worked together in the machine shops and could spend time together in the prison library. Lawson studied in the library, using books that had been provided by church groups and the families of inmates, and he formed a study group with five white draft resistors. Calling themselves a "cell group," they would gather in the library four to five times a week for conversation, prayer, and study at six o'clock in the morning.

Many of the white prisoners were hostile toward the African American inmates, and they were also suspicious of draft resistors. As a result, Lawson and the five draft resistors were labeled "troublemakers."[17] Eight months later they were transferred to the federal penitentiary in Ashland, Kentucky, where Lawson was placed in maximum custody. Lawson could have avoided prison by applying for exemption from the draft as a minister or a student, but he was motivated by his belief in the importance of resisting unfair laws and practices.

Lawson served thirteen months in prison before being paroled in 1952. After his release, he moved to Nagpur, India. This decision was based on three considerations. First, Lawson recalled, "As I went through college I was of the mind that I wanted to live elsewhere than the United States, to see both what that meant to my understanding of my religious practice and as an American."[18] Second, although he had applied to a mission in Africa during his senior year of college, Lawson could not attend because of his arrest record. David Moses, president of Nagpur's Hislop College, invited him to be a campus minister and to teach physical education at the school. Third, Lawson admired Gandhi and his nation's struggle for freedom. "I chose to go to India deliberately," he says, "because [of] Gandhi and Nehru and . . . to meet people who were a part of the Gandhian movement towards independence."[19] Lawson's study of nonviolence in the United States compelled him to explore India on many levels, as he "counted Gandhi as one of my intellectual and spiritual mentor[s]."[20]

Lawson's experiences in India contributed to the development of his own philosophy of nonviolence. "I was able to visit ashrams of Gandhi, pick up books that were not available in the US," he noted. "And I even had a chance to visit with Prime Minister Nehru, the first prime minister of India, who was . . . perhaps the best democrat of the twentieth century."[21] Gandhi had been dead for five years, and Lawson's experiences in India showed him that the nonviolence movement had become fragmented. Nonetheless, he studied the creative strategies of nonviolence that had overthrown British imperialism with the intention of applying the lessons at home.

Lawson's time outside the United States allowed him to step back and critically evaluate American policies. His studies in India shaped his perspective on nonviolence, race, and oppression.[22] In his biography of Lawson, Ernest M. Limbo states that Gandhi saw the conflict between oppressed people of color and their white oppressors as a "global injustice," and Limbo notes that this led Lawson to "understand the plight of blacks in America as but one example of the global oppression of nonwhite peoples."[23] The Southeast Asian Treaty Organization (SEATO) was formed while Lawson was in India, and he recalled that India, under Nehru's leadership, declined to join.

In December 1955 Lawson read about the Montgomery bus boycott in the *Nagpur Times*.[24] He was elated. The very principles of nonviolent resistance that he was studying were being used to oppose Jim Crow customs and laws in Montgomery in a campaign led by a young black minister named Martin Luther King Jr.[25] "Gandhi had said that perhaps the Negro people could lift nonviolence up for the world to see in a way that he could not," Lawson observed. "By '53, I decided that one of the places where I would work one day was in the South and, quite specifically, as a kind of mission field for nonviolence."[26] Lawson decided that his next step would be to return to the United States, where he could work to desegregate the South through church-based activism and community organizing.

When his three-year assignment in India ended in April 1956, Lawson traveled through Africa for six weeks, visiting West Africa, Uganda, Kenya, Tanzania, Rwanda, Congo, Ghana, Nigeria, Sierra Leone, and Liberia. In Africa he witnessed not only the blatant role of US neocolonial policy but also ongoing movements for self-determination, just as he had seen in India. He also observed the role of Christian missionaries who viewed African people as uncivilized.

In August 1956, upon his return to the United States, Lawson enrolled in Oberlin College's Graduate School of Theology. Here he had the opportunity to talk with King. The director of the campus YMCA, Harvey Cox (who became a well-known theologian), was fascinated by King and had invited the young minister to present a daylong series of lectures in February 1957. The speeches, which attracted many students and Ohio residents, included "The Montgomery Story," "Justice without Violence," which was on Gandhian principles, and "The New Negro in the New South."[27]

Cox made certain that Lawson was at a private luncheon for King that followed the morning session because he knew of their shared interests. "Martin King and I had got there first, so we immediately started talking," Lawson recalled.[28] Encouraged by Lawson's extensive knowledge of nonviolence, King urged Lawson to move to the South to pursue a more active role in the movement. King told Lawson that he was the only American activist with such far-reaching knowledge of Gandhian tactics.[29] At King's insistence, Lawson dropped out of graduate school. Lawson spoke with Muste and was offered a position as the FOR's southern secretary. He was planning to finish the semester and begin his new job in the fall of 1957, but in April he fell ill with appendicitis. Lawson said that he knew at the time that his focus would have to be on self-care: "Healing is more important than anything else."[30]

Lawson began his position with FOR in January 1958. He had the option of working in Atlanta, where the African American community was highly organized. The National Association for the Advancement of Colored People (NAACP), for example, had office space, a large membership base, a set leadership, and a set way of thinking. Instead, Lawson chose Nashville so that he could attend Vanderbilt Divinity School, which was known for having the best theology program in the South. Nashville also presented opportunities that were not available in Atlanta, given Atlanta's conventional politics. In addition, Lawson already knew people in Nashville, including members of the Methodist church who had supported him while he was in prison. Lawson moved to Nashville in January 1958.

On the surface, Tennessee appeared to have less racial animus than other Southern states such as Mississippi and Alabama. Tennessee's two senators had refused to sign the "Southern Manifesto," a document issued by ninety-six senators from eleven states in the South that declared that the US Supreme Court's decision in *Brown v. Board of Education* was an abuse of judicial power. Tennessee's governor, Frank G. Clement, was far more moderate than other Southern politicians, and there were a number of successful African American colleges in Nashville.[31] Nashville, and unquestionably the rest of Tennessee, was less flexible than it appeared, however. The majority of African American families lived below the poverty line, and segregation was a way of life in churches, hospitals, restaurants, schools, and theaters.

Although Lawson was based in Nashville, his FOR field assignments necessitated travel throughout the South so that he could personally share his teachings on nonviolence. One of his first projects was to support the Little Rock 9, nine African American students who had been prevented from attending Little Rock Central High School in Little Rock, Arkansas, despite a federal order to desegregate the city's public schools. Lawson held nonviolence workshops in Little Rock from January through May 1958. The first workshop was in the living room of Daisy Bates, the president of the Arkansas State Conference of the NAACP. Lawson met with students and supporters two to three days a week. At one point there were more than one hundred attendees, including white students, parents, and some administrators who supported the Little Rock 9, as well as other African American students who were seeking admission to the high school. Carlotta Walls, one of the Little Rock 9, told Lawson that she had been the target of "bombs"—spitballs filled with metal, stones, and wood—that had been thrown by hostile white students, and the two had a brainstorming session about how she could respond with kindness.[32] While Lawson's focus was on teaching nonviolence, he also emphasized building relationships to advance the movement. For example, Lawson invited King to attend the graduation ceremony of Ernest Green, the first of the Little Rock 9 to complete high school.

In 1958, Lawson attended his first meeting of the Southern Christian Leadership Conference (SCLC) in Columbia, South Carolina, where he met with King and led his first workshop on nonviolence. SCLC leaders invited him to travel throughout the South to attend meetings, lead workshops, plan campaigns, and counsel emerging community and student leaders. "I travel a great deal, preaching, speaking, lecturing, and advising local groups in the fields of Christian peace-making and reconciliation in race relations," he wrote to a Nashville resident in 1958.[33] He visited Raleigh, Greensboro, Charlottesville, Jackson, Memphis, Louisville, and Birmingham. During his workshops Lawson would share a popular comic book about the Montgomery bus boycott, which had been developed by FOR to spread the lessons of nonviolence.

Lawson's work in 1958 marked the beginning of his role as a national leader in the series of desegregation campaigns that later became known as the civil rights movement. In Nashville, Lawson and Rev. Glenn Smiley taught a workshop on nonviolence in March that was sponsored by Rev. Kelly Miller Smith and the Nashville Christian Leadership Council (NCLC), a chapter of the SCLC. In May, Lawson met Dorothy Wood, the secretary of the National Council of Churches for Christ. They shared a common commitment to the church and to the desegregation movement. When the two of them went to a performance of the Nashville Symphony, they were ushered from their orchestra seats to a section for African Americans in the balcony. They went back downstairs and informally desegregated Symphony Hall that night.[34] The two married the next year.

Lawson enrolled in Vanderbilt Divinity School in September 1958. Resolved to plan and implement a nonviolent direct action campaign in Nashville, in 1959 Lawson and leaders of the NCLC began holding regular Saturday meetings with an intergenerational group of community members who were determined to desegregate the city. These meetings began in January and continued into June. The group, which included C. T. Vivian and Dolores Wilkenson, determined the type of campaign they would use, and Lawson planned the strategy for the campaign. Preparing the group for direct action began with a set of workshops that started in September 1959. These workshops included Marion Barry, Jim Bevel, Pauline Knight, Bernard Lafayette, John Lewis, and Diane Nash, as well as Vivian and Wilkenson. Momentum increased in February 1960 when the campaign organizers went public and the workshops grew in size.

In February 1960 the Nashville sit-in campaign was launched. The goal was to desegregate downtown Nashville. During the third week of the campaign Lawson and other leaders of the sit-in campaign were arrested along with dozens of students, and the resulting controversy affected Lawson's graduate studies at Vanderbilt University. On March 3, 1960, the executive trustees of the university expelled Lawson, and the dean of the divinity school and members of the school's faculty resigned in support, sparking a national debate.[35] *The New York Times* asked "whether or not the university can be identified with a continuing campaign of mass disobedience of law as a means of protest."[36] The lunch counters in downtown Nashville were officially desegregated on May 10, 1960, and Lawson continued to work full time in the city until June.

The month before, Lawson had collaborated with Ella Baker, Martin Luther King Jr., and other SCLC members to found the Student Nonviolent Coordinating Committee (SNCC). Three cars of Nashville student activists attended the first SNCC conference, held that month at Shaw University in Raleigh. The recently expelled Lawson was the keynote speaker.[37]

After the Nashville sit-in campaign, Lawson moved to Boston, where he completed his degree at Boston University in August 1960. He then returned to Tennessee, taking a position as a pastor at Scott Methodist Church in Shelbyville, fifty miles from Nashville. He also worked as the director of nonviolent education for the SCLC, a volunteer position that King had asked him to fill. This work took him throughout the South, where he presented educational programs and supported a series of nonviolent campaigns. When the Freedom Ride buses were attacked in Alabama in 1961, Lawson, Nash, and others from the Nashville sit-in movement lent their support. Lawson even held a workshop on nonviolence inside one of the buses after it was attacked in Montgomery.[38] Lawson also staffed Birmingham's 1963 desegregation campaign in partnership with Fred Shuttlesworth, a minister and co-founder of the SCLC. In the summer of 1964, Lawson participated in the Mississippi Summer campaign to register African American voters in the face of fierce efforts by white elected officials and law enforcement agents to block African Americans' access to the polls.

Rev. James M. Lawson Jr. and Dorothy Wood Lawson on their wedding day. *Courtesy of Rev. James M. Lawson Jr.*

Lawson became pastor of the Centenary Methodist Church in Memphis in 1962. As pastor, Lawson participated in struggles for justice locally, nationally, and internationally.[39] When the United States began escalating its involvement in the Vietnam War, Lawson engaged in debates within the SCLC that focused on whether to oppose the war. King and Lawson publicly spoke out against the United States' role in Vietnam, challenging other clergy and leaders of the SCLC and the community who saw this as a distraction from the focus on civil rights.

In May 1965 Lawson received a call from King, who asked Lawson to join a peace-seeking mission to Vietnam and Southeast Asia in his place. That summer Lawson left for a six-week tour of Cambodia, South Vietnam, Hong Kong, and Australia. Lawson met with officials at the US embassy, journalists from *Time*, and Buddhist spiritual leader Thich Nhat Hanh. Lawson reported back to the National Council of Churches in Australia and prepared reports for the SCLC and FOR that condemned US involvement in the war.

In 1968 Lawson assumed an instrumental leadership position in the Memphis sanitation workers' strike. Two black sanitation workers were killed on the job during a rainstorm in February. In response, nearly thirteen thousand sanitation workers walked out to protest unsafe conditions and unequal treatment. Workers decried the city's racially discriminatory labor policies, which denied African American workers paid time off during poor weather conditions while providing it for their white coworkers. On February 23 the police broke up a peaceful march using handheld canisters of mace. This was the first time that mace had been used against civilians at a peaceful protest in the United States.[40] In response, African American community leaders formed a strategy committee to explore forging an alliance between the workers and the community, and Lawson was named the chair.[41] He conducted nonviolence workshops for sanitation workers and their community allies. To advance the demand that all humans be treated with dignity, the workers adopted the slogan I Am a Man.

The committee called for daily picket lines in Memphis, organized mass meetings, and asked Rev. Harold Middlebrook, also a member of the SCLC, to organize high school students to join the picket lines in the late afternoons and early evenings. Later the committee called for an economic boycott of downtown Memphis to step up pressure on the business community and elected officials. They invited prominent leaders, including Rustin, King, and NAACP leader Roy Wilkins, to lend their support. On the evening of April 3, 1968, King delivered his famous "Mountaintop" speech, in which he called for the fair treatment of Memphis's sanitation workers and commended Lawson, the campaign, and the use of nonviolent tactics.[42] He was assassinated the next day at the Lorraine Motel in Memphis. The sanitation workers prevailed and a settlement was signed on April 16. The city agreed to recognize the union and to improve wages and working conditions. The campaign signaled an advancement in forging stronger partnerships between labor and the civil rights movement. In July of that year, Lawson attended the general assembly of the World Council of Churches in Uppsala, Sweden, where he represented the nonviolent desegregation movement. King had also been scheduled to attend.

In 1969, Lawson supported a hospital strike for black workers in Memphis. He also participated in the Black Monday protests, held to draw attention to employment discrimination and educational inequity in Memphis. The protests, which began in October, included marches and boycotts of schools and businesses that involved tens of thousands of Memphis citizens. In December, Lawson was one of several African American leaders who were arrested for their involvement, and he spent Christmas in jail.

Rev. Ezekiel Bell, Rev. Henry L. Starks, Jerry Wurf (president of the American Federation of State, County, and Municipal Employees), and Rev. James M. Lawson Jr. (right to left) at a rally during the Memphis sanitation strike, 1968. *Courtesy of Walter P. Reuther Library, Archives of Labor and Urban Affairs, Wayne State University.*

Rev. James M. Lawson Jr. addresses a racially mixed crowd during an event on April 7, 1968, three days after the assassination of Rev. Martin Luther King Jr. The event, called "Memphis Cares," was held at Memphis's Crump Stadium. *Courtesy of Preservation and Special Collections, University Libraries, University of Memphis.*

Lawson continued in his volunteer role with the SCLC through 1972. He participated in peace vigils for the Vietnam War and efforts to desegregate the United Methodist Church. He led a World Council of Churches committee that focused on violence and nonviolence in the struggle for justice; this role, which he held until 1972, took him to meetings across the country. He was also busy with his pastoral duties, which included moving his congregation to a new facility.

Lawson moved to Los Angeles in 1974 and began his twenty-five-year tenure as pastor of Holman United Methodist Church. He participated in marches and meetings against the Vietnam War. He was appointed the president of the local SCLC chapter and, in 1977, the vice president of SCLC West. He continued to build interfaith coalitions for peace and justice. He led Peace Sunday, a large antiwar benefit at the Rose Bowl, in June 1982, various antinuclear efforts throughout the 1980s, and peace committees that opposed US policy in El Salvador, Nicaragua, and Guatemala. Lawson traveled to El Salvador, where he met with members of the Sandinista National Liberation Front. In 1982 he spoke before 125,000 people at rally against nuclear armament in Berlin. He recalls that at the time he was "a pastor at a church and considered this all of what a pastor should be engaged in."[43] In Los Angeles Lawson participated in a campaign to rename Santa Barbara Avenue to Martin Luther King Jr. Boulevard. As a part of an interfaith task force on hunger, he advocated for fresh farm produce and helped organize the Adams/Vermont farmers' market in South Los Angeles.

In the late 1980s and 1990s Lawson participated in the Los Angeles labor movement, teaching the principles and tactics of nonviolence to organizers in the hotel and custodial industries. Maria Elena Durazo, president of Hotel Employees and Restaurant Employees International Union (HERE) Local 11, the hotel workers' union, contacted Lawson and asked him to educate her staff and members on the philosophy of nonviolence. Durazo, who came from a family of farmworkers, had organized with the United Farm Workers (UFW). She invited Lawson and UFW president César Chávez to speak to hotel workers in the early 1990s and to advise the union on a campaign against the Hyatt Hotel in downtown Los Angeles. Lawson asked her, "How do we do in LA what we did in Memphis? How do we engender church support for union organizing?"[44] In 1996 Lawson helped found the Clergy and Laity United for Economic Justice (CLUE-LA), an interfaith organization focused on worker justice, which continues to mobilize the faith-based community to actively support immigrant and workers' rights.[45]

Like his workshops in Nashville and Memphis, the nonviolence training that Lawson offered in Los Angeles was grounded in a philosophical and moral understanding of the potential of nonviolent struggle to improve the lives of workers. "I got arrested for labor struggles more in Los Angeles than I ever did in the Civil Rights Movement," Lawson noted.[46] This pioneering work to introduce nonviolence to hotel workers was instrumental in the transformation of the labor movement in Los Angeles.

Lawson participated in the 2003 immigrant workers' Freedom Ride, in which immigrants traveled by bus from Los Angeles and other major US cities to the New York area. The Freedom Ride culminated in a rally in New Jersey's Liberty State Park, across the harbor from the Statue of Liberty. Lawson, speaking at a related demonstration in Flushing Meadows Park, proclaimed, "Every man and every woman has a right for jobs with dignity, for safety at work, for families being united and able to support themselves and sustain themselves in a living and meaningful fashion."[47] The event mobilized labor and community partnerships for immigrant rights throughout the country.

Lawson continues to have a profound impact on social justice organizations locally and nationally. He has taught the philosophy of nonviolence to students working for the passage of a federal DREAM Act. Their groundbreaking direct actions have brought about changes in immigration policy at state and federal levels.[48]

LAWSON'S LESSONS ON THE PHILOSOPHY OF NONVIOLENCE

Lawson begins his workshops on nonviolence by providing a grounding in its history. He points out that "nonviolence is a twentieth-century concept" conceived by Gandhi in 1906, when he was a young lawyer in South Africa. Gandhi was traveling by train from Natal to Pretoria in a first-class compartment when he was brutally thrown off at Maritzburg by a railway guard and a local police constable. A white passenger had requested his removal because he was a "colored man." Gandhi spent the freezing night on the benches in the station's waiting room, thinking about the experience and the indignity of racial segregation. He recalled the incident in his autobiography: "Should I fight for my rights or go back to India, or should I go on to Pretoria without minding the insults. . . . The hardship to which I was subjected was superficial—only a symptom of the deep disease of color prejudice."[49] Lawson teaches that Gandhi "was so angry, he sat up all night in the cold weather," thinking about how to respond. He puts himself in Gandhi's place and asks, "Do I resist with the same meanness that is being displayed by the problem itself? Do I do it the way the British are imposing?"[50]

Gandhi studied tactics of resistance that would allow him to oppose colonial regimes. He researched models of community struggle, but he could not find an existing concept or term that captured his ideas. He used the term *nonviolence* to convey a type of peaceful resistance that could include militancy. Although Gandhi combated imperialism and segregation through nonpassive, action-oriented resistance, he also sought to root nonviolence in the religious philosophy of *ahimsa,* a Sanskrit term meaning "not to injure." It is an approach embraced by Hinduism and Jainism. Stressing both action and noninjury, Gandhi's method of nonviolence embraces a fundamental respect and love for all living things. The use of nonviolence to eradicate oppression also relies on "love in action." Lawson notes that Gandhi viewed nonviolence as "the greatest force available to human beings at that time—more powerful than electricity, more powerful than any other form of power."[51]

Using Gandhi's and India's struggles against the British Empire as a model, Lawson presents a nuanced analysis of power and violence. First, he describes a focus on power as one distinguishing factor between nonviolence and other forms of resistance such as pacifism. Second, he points out that understanding the use of power requires an understanding of violence. "I define violence in a combined way, from experience," he states. "I see violence as the misuse of power. It is not just done by a fist or a gun or hitting someone over a chair, it is done by economic structures. So there is such a thing as systemic power, structural power."[52] Lawson points to Britain's dominance of India as an example of structural power. Britain controlled not only the nation's legal systems but also its education systems, economic development, and trade, which allowed Britain to control many aspects of people's lives. Lawson evaluates the misuse of power in multiple forms: it operates between individuals, within the economy, and within the political and social systems. Nonviolence challenges the misuse of power, and it also builds power as a source of promoting humanizing change.

Lawson then analyzes power and violence in the context of American history and economics, focusing particularly on "plantation capitalism." He describes how an understanding of power requires an understanding of racism, sexism, and violence in the context of slavery. In plantation capitalism, slaves were treated as a commodity and a form of wealth, and slave women were raped to produce more slaves. According to Lawson, plantation capitalism continues to shape American life—wage theft is one example—and

Power is the capacity to effect purpose. . . .
Power is a given, it's given by creation.
It's given by the gift of life. And it
constitutes a force from the universe itself, from
life itself and **enables you to become human
and alive**! . . . It is the capacity to effect purpose.
—Rev. Lawson April 2013

"represents a misuse of power."[53] Plantation capitalism is a form of violence that the practice of nonviolence helps to dismantle.

Lawson emphasizes practicing love as a key to nonviolence. Love is an often generalized and misinterpreted concept. Lawson interprets Gandhi's understanding of love as encompassing respect, reverence, and trust in life, and he strives to "define love, power, and nonviolence as Gandhi did," in connection with one another. Yet Lawson comprehends love as more than a broad notion of respect. "When I say that a part of the task of nonviolence is to love the enemy," he says, "I mean respecting that your enemy has in his or her DNA, genes, and mind the same stream of life that is in you. If you respect yourself and the gift that is yours of life, then you have to also respect it even in the person that is trying to do you harm."[54] Practicing nonviolence as love is an exercise that is drawn from the narratives of Jesus and the writings of Gandhi and centers on sharing common life forces and not hating or despising others. Lawson points out that this sense of common humanity is always at odds with systemic violence.

Lawson also draws on his studies as a minister to express his interpretation of nonviolence, love, and respect as a process of self-reflection. In his workshops he often points to the book of Matthew, chapters 5 through 7. Matthew 5:38–48 addresses the "eye for an eye" principle as well as the concept of loving your enemy. Lawson recalls that this passage helped him when he experienced racial denigration as an adolescent.

> Jesus is saying, though these are not his words but my paraphrase, if you live in the Roman Empire, which is a pretty terrible occupation of our land, you do not have to become a Roman Empire supporter. You do not have to act that way. You have a kind of singular autonomy that you can decide you're going to resist the wrongdoer, the evildoer. You're not going to retaliate.[55]

This passage was a strategic "tool kit" that was especially useful in junior and senior high school. Lawson's interpretation of the passage promotes nonviolent resistance as a way to challenge empires and occupation. He views Gandhi as close to Jesus in his everyday approach of nonviolent resistance.[56]

Over the decades Lawson has linked the teachings of Gandhi and Jesus to the US experience, creating a practical tool kit that allows his students to embrace a life that is ever-focused on justice. Lawson uses Mathew 5:38–48 as a training tool to help his participants identify their personal power. Personal power can be used to either employ or reject violence and oppression. He encourages self-reflection to assess the types of actions that perpetuate cycles of violence. Lawson's approach relies on personal analysis. His students choose to be "autonomous"—they choose to resist the perpetration of wrongdoing.[57] "You can decide to be a non-cooperator with a wrongful social scene, decide that you will not support racism or sexism in your society," he points out.[58]

The workshops that Lawson presented during the 1960s offered something larger than "know-how" to many of his students. Lawson taught his participants how to build power in a campaign through love and transformation in addition to direct action, and he allowed them to explore their own fears in the face of violence. For example, Lawson remembers reading Luke 4:14–31 to demonstrate how to control anger in the midst of a potentially violent action. Lawson describes Jesus as a first-century human being who had to walk through a mob that was ready to throw him over a cliff. By focusing, Jesus was able to walk through the crowd without incident.

Lawson's philosophy of nonviolence was tested during the formative years of the civil rights movement. Lafayette was one of Lawson's students during the Nashville sit-ins. He later became a key leader in the SNCC, along with Bevel, Nash, and Lewis. In an interview in 2013, Lafayette stressed the importance of Lawson's approach to nonviolence.

> There are many kinds of nonviolent teachings and trainings. So if a person says, 'I have been through nonviolent trainings,' that might not tell you a lot. What was different, uniquely, about the training that Jim Lawson did, it gave you an opportunity to discover within yourself a power that you didn't realize you had.[59]

Rev. James M. Lawson Jr. speaks to hotel workers in Los Angeles during HERE Local 11's campaign against the New Otani Hotel in 1996. *Courtesy of HERE Local 11.*

At first many of Lawson's students found controlling their anger and loving the enemy inconceivable, as Lafayette noted: "How are you going to love your enemy?. . . It was not just tactics. It was a change that had to take place within us. . . . Could we in fact allow someone to slap us?"[60] He recalled how he soon learned to control the urges of anger in the midst of racial violence. Rather than being provoked by physical violence, Lafayette found a new sense of power when he chose not to react with violence.

As they prepared for the Nashville sit-in campaign, Lawson's students internalized these lessons on the philosophy and actions of Jesus, Gandhi, and King. After the campaign ended, they carried the philosophy of nonviolence with them as they embarked on other desegregation campaigns in the South. Many of the leaders of the Nashville campaign assumed new leadership roles at the second SNCC conference, held October 14–16, 1960, at Atlanta University. Lawson, Baker, and King were featured speakers. The conference theme, "Nonviolence and the Achievement of Desegregation," reflected the prominence of nonviolence strategies within the movement.[61]

The SNCC's first student newspaper, *The Student Voice*, shows the impact of Lawson's philosophy on the desegregation movement. In the December 1960 issue, a statement titled "The Damage of Fear and the Promise of Love" describes a Ku Klux Klan rally in Atlanta, a nitroglycerin attack at an African American elementary school, and the climate of increasing fear that resulted. The statement had been drafted by the participants at the SNCC's founding conference at Shaw University in April 1960. Nearly 120 participants provided input to the statement, demonstrating the reach of Lawson's teachings.

> We affirm the philosophical or religious ideal of nonviolence as the foundation of our purpose, the presupposition of our faith, and the manner of our action. Nonviolence, as it grows from Judaic-Christian traditions, seeks a social order of justice permeated by love. Integration of human endeavor represents the first step towards such a society. Through nonviolence, courage displaces fear, love transforms hate. Acceptance dissipates prejudice; hope ends despair. Peace dominates war; faith reconciles doubt. Mutual regard cancels enmity. Justice for all overthrows injustice. . . . Love is the eternal motif of nonviolence. . . . Such love goes to the extreme: it remains loving and forgiving even in the midst of hostility.[62]

The SNCC students could envision a future without prejudice, despair, war, or doubt because nonviolence had the power to alleviate the fear that was triggered by everyday violence and racial injustice.

Lawson teaches his students that loving yourself and loving the people who participate in the struggle for nonviolence with you is key to imagining a world free of violence and oppression. He believes that during the struggle for justice in the 1960s, the way his students interacted with one another, the way the vision of the nonviolence movement was implemented, and the way that the participants came together shaped a collective spirit of nonviolence, in which "the means and the ends [were] interwoven."[63]

LAWSON'S METHODS FOR A NONVIOLENT CAMPAIGN

Lawson's philosophy of nonviolence has been a core element of social justice movements for more than five decades, and his methods have been incorporated into campaigns throughout the country. He first began to test his principles of nonviolence in 1958, as part of the community-based campaign that led to the Nashville sit-ins. He realized the urgency of building on the lessons of the Montgomery bus boycott, an understanding shared by his colleagues at the SCLC and FOR. Lawson held a series of workshops on nonviolence, examined the segregated conditions in Nashville and the South, and conducted participatory strategy meetings. He then began adapting Gandhi's philosophy into a set of practical methods.

In Nashville, Lawson tested methods that shifted the political landscape of the South and advanced strategic nonviolence to the forefront of the desegregation movement. The Nashville plan drew from a knowledge of practical conditions and involved creative experimentation. He remembers that he was "quite confident that we could subject a Southern city to nonviolent campaign that would make a difference, . . . that what happened in Montgomery with King developing the notion that a nonviolent movement could be repeated. What the form of that was, I did not know."[64]

The methods that Lawson tested in Nashville became a core part of the curriculum of strategy, role-playing, active resistance, and transformation that he teaches today. Lawson's workshops on nonviolence include training in his four steps for a nonviolent campaign and the use of nonviolent tactics, and lessons on the philosophy of nonviolence and the history of the nonviolence movement. The four steps, which have evolved over the years, are:

1. Focus,
2. Negotiation,
3. Direct action, and
4. Follow-up.[65]

tools in campaigns for social justice (handwritten annotation)

Lawson developed his four steps from ten steps that encompass Gandhi's teachings:

1. Investigation,
2. Negotiation and arbitration,
3. Preparation of the group for direct action,
4. Agitation,
5. Issuing an ultimatum,
6. Economic boycott and forms of strike,
7. Non-cooperation,
8. Civil disobedience,
9. Usurping functions of the government, and
10. Parallel government.[66]

In his workshops Lawson always presents these ten steps to honor Gandhi and to establish why he is considered the father of nonviolence.

Lawson's four steps serve as practitioners' tools in campaigns for social justice. The first step, focus, includes the essential groundwork for a campaign. Lawson emphasizes that, first and foremost, practitioners must understand the main issues and problems at hand in order to evaluate and set priorities. Once the issue is identified, the first step involves conducting research thoroughly to "learn all you can." Research requires practitioners to educate others by sharing their findings, which will help build a community of activists who can prepare for nonviolent direct action. Next, practitioners determine an ultimate goal or vision, shape a strategy, develop a calendar for the campaign, and educate the public. Lawson advises organizers to "launch nonviolent training, adopt common discipline for the struggle, and develop the negotiations plan and team" as part of step one. Recruitment is also an essential element of step one. Lastly, this first step stresses creating a media network as a way "to win the public."[67]

Rev. James M. Lawson Jr. lecturing at a graduate seminar at the University of California, Los Angeles, on May 8, 2013. *Courtesy of Pocho Sanchez.*

Lawson's second step is negotiation. The first step continues while the second step begins. Lawson says that negotiation engages the target of the campaign: "Know your opponent and plan to educate them for the larger picture and vision." The second step includes informing the opponent about the grievance and drafting an agreement for all parties to sign. Furthermore, a key element of the negotiation process is perfecting the calendar and the plan for direct action. Campaign demands and timely ultimatums should be offered. This step also includes demonstrations that function as a starting point for the direct action. Lawson states that these demonstrations, which begin to apply pressure while negotiation is underway, are "an excellent way to continue your training."[68] Another component of this step is concerned with preparing for legal action by addressing the potential for charges against protestors, securing bail money, and formulating a provision to drop charges against protestors as a part of a negotiated agreement.

Step three, direct action, involves the development of creative, action-oriented nonviolent tactics that will "make the situation unmanageable for the opponents." In this step Lawson tells participants to "prepare for a protracted struggle (nonviolent warfare)" and suggests moving from "simple weapons to the more complex." The success of step three relies on the continuation of teaching about nonviolent direct action, recruiting, and training. It also relies on inspiration, which can be encouraged by holding meetings that will renew participants' commitment and encourage community support. Lawson stresses the importance of discipline and advises leaders to reject actions from those who "do their own thing." The last part of this step addresses amplification of the goal through direct action: "You explain your movement directly to the public" and "let the press come to you."[69] Lawson recommends testing the direct action campaign to improve and perfect its focus, and he notes that this step does not preclude continued work on the first and second steps.

Step four, follow-up, is centered on conclusion and accountability. It covers the conclusion of negotiations, which require "a signed written agreement with a calendar" that specifies when new policies will be initiated. Lawson advises leaders to have a structure for follow-up in place and a way to "educate the movement and larger community about the agreement." The fourth step also addresses any "repair work" that might be necessary and a de-escalation of the direct action campaign: "Work at the reconciliation tasks, follow up on opponents who changed and want change, and be sure they have adequate support for your future." This last step encourages outreach and leadership development in addition to the continuation of training and direct action, along with a strong implementation and evaluation plan for the campaign. Lawson notes that the last step should serve as a transition to the next campaign, where leaders "move back toward" the first step and "select the next target."[70]

An essential element of Lawson's workshops is training in nonviolent tactics, which includes a practical exercise in which participants role-play their responses to violence. In Nashville Lawson used role-playing to prepare activists for possible violent confrontations. He would ask two people to stand at the front of the room. One person would be tasked with verbally assaulting or even slapping the other person to determine how the first person would respond to being verbally or physically attacked. Lawson knew that the protestors had to be "realistic about facing violence."[71] Lafayette concurred, recalling his own experiences in Lawson's workshops.

> The purpose here in the training was to give emotional conditioning. because it's one thing to tell someone intellectually, you know, "You're going to go down and you're not going to hit back." But to take them through a role play where someone would slap you and push you . . . The thing that was so amazing to me is, our role play is exactly what happened when we got down there.[72]

Lafayette described how Lawson stressed confronting physical violence rather than hiding from it.

> Now, Jim Lawson did not teach us to roll up into a ball and put our heads over, like that. . . . That's what I mean by there was a difference in the nonviolence trainings. Some people were telling folks to do that. . . . He trained us to confront the people and to face our opponents. . . . So what you are doing is rather than reacting and allowing them to control your behavior, so you are retaliating. What you are doing is giving the better example. You are turning the other cheek. They are showing how ugly they could react towards you and you are trying to show how loving that you can act towards them.[73]

Facing opponents rather than turning away humanized both the attacker and the resister, and allowed the students to retain power during the attack. Even in the midst of violence students had to rely on love to maintain power, respect, and dignity. Lawson taught his students to use *agape* (the Greek word for love) to form community with a sense of purpose and graciousness. Lawson's Nashville students carried this tool of agape with them as they led other nonviolent campaigns in the years that followed. Role-playing was one of the most transformative components of Lawson's nonviolence training during the Nashville campaign.

Lawson also includes political education in his workshops, in which he discusses racial injustice, oppression, and structural violence. He draws from examples of the Montgomery bus boycott, Gandhi's march to protest the British salt tax, the Polish solidarity

Bernard Lafayette and Rev. James M. Lawson Jr. at a graduate seminar at the University of California, Los Angeles, on May 8, 2013. *Courtesy of Pocho Sanchez.*

movement, and the South African struggle against apartheid. Lawson incorporates lessons of resistance in the larger context of overcoming systemic oppression and injustice.

THE BELOVED COMMUNITY AND NONVIOLENCE TODAY

Lawson's goal for his workshop participants is for them to embrace their own power through practice. He states, "Gandhi said that nonviolence cannot be taught. It has to be practiced, it has to be lived."[74] Lawson's training in nonviolence fosters a sense of empowerment. "It's power, but it's a different kind of power," he explains. "When you have the power because of your own transformation to help the other person change, that's what I call real power."[75]

Gandhi believed in the "science of nonviolence" as a method for achieving social justice that could also be embraced as a personal way of living, working, and acting.[76] Lawson's first workshops in Nashville engaged participants in a study of nonviolence as a science and as a way of life. To this day, he continues to emphasize his conviction that nonviolence is a social science that can activate change. Lawson teaches that nonviolence promotes a vision of a just world not only through the study of its tenets but also through the practice of building a movement. Lafayette noted that Lawson's nonviolence training showed "that you have the power to effect those kinds of changes." As a result, Lafayette said, "you were not feeling helpless, pitiful. You were not feeling alone."[77]

Lawson's life journey to "find another way" to address segregation and racial violence led him to the study of nonviolence. His study of Jesus and Gandhi and his friendship and collaboration with Martin Luther King Jr. paved the way for his pivotal role as a teacher and philosopher of nonviolence grounded in the US experience. Vivian, a fellow civil rights veteran, said that Lawson's workshops "made all the difference in the world. Not only that it put a whole group of us in terms of exposure to nonviolence as methodology, it put us way ahead of our time in the United States in the Southern region. Other people never had that knowledge or that experience."[78]

Through his teachings, Lawson creates the space for the "beloved community" advocated by King. The philosophy of nonviolence as "love in action" seeks to foster a "community of love where all persons will have a similar opportunity to grow towards their God-given capacities."[79] In his work in Nashville, Lawson "stressed the Gandhian idea of our being engaged in an experiment." He recalls that it was a process of transformation: "In an experiment, you have to keep figuring out what happened, and why, and what didn't happen. And you have to lay the framework for allowing the experiment to help you to the next step."[80] Nonviolent power is a creative universal force for fostering justice. Lawson's philosophy of nonviolence has led generations of activists through a process of personal reflection, transformation, and love.

NOTES

This chapter draws extensively from interviews of Rev. Lawson and guest speakers that were held during a special topics course sponsored by the Labor Center, the César E. Chávez Department of Chicana/o Studies, the Labor and Workplace Studies Minor, the Department of African American Studies, and the History Department at UCLA. Martin Luther King Jr.'s speeches, letters, and other documents are available online through the King Papers Project at Stanford University; http://mlk-kpp01.stanford.edu/primarydocuments/Vol4/3-Nov-1958_FromLawson.pdf.

1. According to Lawson, he and King spoke then, only a month after the Montgomery bus boycott had ended on January 18, 1957. James Lawson, interview by Preeti Sharma and Ana Luz González, July 7, 2014, Los Angeles.

2. Quoted in David Halberstam, *The Children* (New York: Random House, 1998), 16. See also Lawson, interview by Sharma and González, July 7, 2014.

3. Lawson insists that on the ground and in the moment, no one was referring to the set of actions, strategies, and organizing as a part of a "civil rights movement." Lawson, interview by Sharma and González, July 7, 2014.

4. Faith Project, Inc., "James Lawson," *This Far By Faith: African American Spiritual Journeys* website, 2003, http://www.pbs.org/thisfarbyfaith/witnesses/james_lawson.html.

5. James M. Lawson Jr., discussion with Kent Wong and Kelly Lytle Hernandez, April 3, 2013, Los Angeles.

6. Lawson says that although Ohio was desegregated at the time, he remembers hearing about local lynchings and confronting other moments of prejudice, violence, and general racism. Lawson, interview by Sharma and González, July 7, 2014.

7. Lawson, discussion with Wong and Lytle Hernandez.

8. Ibid.

9. Peter Ackerman and Jack Duvall, *A Force More Powerful: A Century of Nonviolent Conflict* (New York: Palgrave, 2000), 308, state that Lawson sat in a hamburger joint with a high school friend; Lawson recollects that he sat at a counter in Long's. Lawson, interview by Sharma and González, July 7, 2014.

10. FOR was founded by a British Quaker and a German Lutheran who met at a Christian conference for members of different denominations in December 1914, just as World War I was beginning; the two pledged to remain friends and to refuse to fight in the war that had broken out between their countries. The US chapter of FOR was founded in 1915. FOR grew to be an interfaith, international organization across fifty countries. See Fellowship of Reconciliation, "History of the Fellowship of Reconciliation," FOR website, http://forusa.org/about/history.

11. James M. Lawson Jr., "Interview: Rev. James Lawson," *Nashville 1960: We Were Warriors*, part 1 of *A Force More Powerful: A Century of Nonviolent Conflict*, broadcast on PBS, September 18, 2000,

http://web.archive.org/web/20041209111131/http://www.pbs.org/weta/forcemorepowerful/nashville/interview.html.

12. Ackerman and Duvall, *A Force More Powerful*, 307.

13. The Freedom Rides were conceived by members of FOR and CORE. CORE was founded in 1942. See Congress of Racial Equality, "The History of CORE," CORE website, http://www.core-online.org/History/history.htm. According to Lawson, because CORE was founded by members of FOR, it was an extension of the older organization.

14. Additionally, Lawson said, the draft boards were often comprised of white businessmen, who would pick African American instead of white men. Lawson, discussion with Wong and Lytle Hernandez.

15. Ibid.

16. Lawson, interview by Sharma and González, July 7, 2014.

17. Ernest M. Limbo, "James Lawson: The Nashville Civil Rights Movement," in *The Human Tradition in the Civil Rights Movement*, ed. Susan M. Glisson (Lanham, MD: Rowman & Littlefield Publishers, 2006), 163.

18. Lawson, discussion with Wong and Lytle Hernandez.

19. Ibid.

20. Lawson, "Interview: Rev. James Lawson."

21. Lawson, discussion with Wong and Lytle Hernandez.

22. Faith Project, Inc., "James Lawson."

23. Limbo, "James Lawson," 162.

24. The *Nagpur Times* was a daily newspaper printed in English. Lawson states that it provided consistent coverage on Martin Luther King Jr. and the Montgomery bus boycotts. Lawson, interview by Sharma and González, July 7, 2014.

25. See Halberstam, *The Children*.

26. Lawson, "Interview: Rev. James Lawson."

27. Ibid.

28. Lawson, interview by Sharma and González, July 7, 2014.

29. See Limbo, "James Lawson," 163.

30. Lawson, interview by Sharma and González, July 7, 2014.

31. David M. Oshinsky, "Freedom Riders," *New York Times*, March 15, 1998, http://www.nytimes.com/books/98/03/15/reviews/980315.15oshinst.html?_r=1.

32. Letter from James M. Lawson Jr. to Pauline Morris, April 25, 1958, FOR I Correspondence–FOR Outgoing 1958 Folder, Box 36, Lawson Papers, Special Collections and University Archives, Heard Library, Vanderbilt University. Quoted in Dennis Dickerson, "James M. Lawson, Jr.: Methodism, Nonviolence and The Civil Rights Movement," *Methodist History* 52, no. 3 (2014): 181.

33. Letter from James M. Lawson Jr. to Anita House, May 22, 1958, FOR I Correspondence–Outgoing 1958 Folder, Box 36, Lawson Papers, Special Collections and University Archives, Heard Library, Vanderbilt University. Quoted in Dickerson, "James M. Lawson, Jr.," 14.

34. Theo Emery, "Activist Ousted from Vanderbilt Is Back, as a Teacher," *New York Times*, October 4, 2006, http://www.nytimes.com/2006/10/04/education/04lawson.html.

35. Ackerman and Duvall, *A Force More Powerful*, 323; United Press International, "Divinity Dean Out in Racial Protest: Vanderbilt University Aide Resigns Over Refusal to Readmit Negro Student," *New York Times*, May 31, 1960. See also Limbo, "James Lawson," 171–73.

36. "Negroes Press Protest in South, but the Cold Limits Activities," *New York Times*, March 4, 1960.

37. Howard Zinn, *SNCC: The New Abolitionists* (Boston: Beacon Press, [1964]), 33.

38. Ibid., 51. For information about Diane Nash's coordinating role, see Jennifer A. Stollman, "Diane Nash: 'Courage Displaces Fear, Love Transforms Hate': Civil Rights Activism and the Commitment to Nonviolence," in *The Human Tradition in the Civil Rights Movement*, ed. Susan M. Glisson (Lanham, MD: Roman and Littlefield, 2006), 163.

39. The name of the church was changed in 1968 to Centenary United Methodist Church.

40. Michael K. Honey, *Going Down Jericho Road: The Memphis Strike, Martin Luther King's Last Campaign* (New York: Norton, 2007), 203. See also Ben Kamin, *Room 306: The National Story of the Lorraine Motel* (East Lansing: Michigan State University Press, 2012), 46.

41. Lawson explains that at this time African American ministers formed Community on the Move for Equality (COME) to continue to advocate for sanitation workers; the organization was funded from money raised for the strike fund. James M. Lawson Jr., interview by Preeti Sharma and Ana Luz González,

September 4, 2014, Los Angeles. For more details on the formation of COME, see Honey, *Going Down Jericho Road*, chap. 10.

42. Martin Luther King Jr., "I've Been to the Mountaintop" (speech, Memphis, April 3, 1968), King Papers, Martin Luther King Jr. Research and Education Institute, Stanford University, http://mlk-kpp01 .stanford.edu/index.php/encyclopedia/documentsentry/ive_been_to_the_mountaintop.

43. Lawson, interview by Sharma and González, September 4, 2014.

44. Quoted in Helene Slessarev-Jamir, *Prophetic Activism: Progressive Religious Justice Movements in Contemporary America* (New York: New York University Press, 2011), 110–11.

45. For more on CLUE-LA and Lawson, see Slessarev-Jamir, *Prophetic Activism*, 109; and Pierrette Hondagneu-Sotelo, *God's Heart Has No Borders: How Religious Activists Are Working for Immigrant Rights* (Berkeley: University of California Press, 2008), 88.

46. Lawson, interview by Sharma and González, September 4, 2014.

47. Quoted in John J. Goldman, "2003 Freedom Ride Ends with a New York Rally," *Los Angeles Times*, October 5, 2003.

48. See, for example, Jeanne Batalova and Margie McHugh, *DREAM vs. Reality: An Analysis of Potential DREAM Act Beneficiaries* (Washington, DC: Migration Policy Institute, 2010), www.migrationpolicy .org/pubs/DREAM-Insight-July2010.pdf; Michael A. Olivas, "The Political Economy of the DREAM Act and the Legislative Process: A Case Study of Comprehensive Immigration Reform," *Wayne Law Review* 55 (2010): 1757–1810; and Caitlin Patler and Lauren D. Appelbaum, *Reaching the Dream: The Federal DREAM Act, the California Dream Act, and Undocumented Student Activism*, Research and Policy Brief No. 10 (Los Angeles: UCLA Institute for Research on Labor and Employment, 2011).

49. Mohandas K. Gandhi, *An Autobiography: The Story of My Experiments with Truth* (Boston: Beacon Press, 1993), 112, http://articles.latimes.com/2003/oct/05/nation/na-freedom5. Gandhi was also called a "coolie."

50. Lawson, discussion with Wong and Lytle Hernandez.

51. Ibid.

52. Ibid.

53. James M. Lawson Jr., interview by Preeti Sharma and Ana Luz González, October 15, 2014, Los Angeles.

54. Ibid.

55. Lawson, discussion with Wong and Lytle Hernandez.

56. See Halberstam, *The Children*, 49.

57. Lawson said, "You can also do this inwardly, even if you have shackles on your feet." Lawson, interview by Sharma and González, July 7, 2014.

58. Ibid. Lawson pointed out that "social oppression is a form of tyranny. Structural poverty is social and economic tyranny."

59. James M. Lawson Jr. and Bernard Lafayette, discussion with Kent Wong and Kelly Lytle Hernandez, April 24, 2013, Los Angeles.

60. Ibid.

61. "SNCC Conference," *The Student Voice* 1, no. 3 (1960): 1, http://www.crmvet.org/docs/sv /sv6010.pdf.

62. "The Damage of Fear and the Promise of Love," *The Student Voice* 1, no. 5 (1960): 2.

63. Lawson, interview by Sharma and González, September 4, 2014.

64. Lawson, discussion with Wong and Lytle Hernandez.

65. James M. Lawson Jr., "The Nonviolent Method (as Taught from the 1950s with Great Indebtedness to Gandhi and the Nonviolent Movement, 1955–1975)," handout, 2001.

66. Joan Bondurant distilled Gandhi's work into nine steps in the late 1950s, leaving out "investigation." Lawson came across Bondurant's work in the 1970s. When Lawson developed his ten steps, he reinstated Gandhi's first step, investigation. See Joan V. Bondurant, *Conquest of Violence: The Gandhian Philosophy of Conflict* (Princeton, NJ: Princeton University Press, 1958), 40–41; see also James M. Lawson Jr., "A Comparative View of the Nonviolent System from Three Perspectives," handout, undated.

67. Lawson, "Nonviolent Method."

68. Ibid.

69. Ibid.

70. Ibid.

71. Lawson and Lafayette, discussion with Wong and Lytle Hernandez.

72. Ibid.

73. Ibid.

74. James M. Lawson Jr., discussion with Carlos Amador, Sofia Campos, Neidi Dominguez, and Kent Wong, May 8, 2013, Los Angeles.

75. Lawson and Lafayette, discussion with Wong and Lytle Hernandez.

76. Mohandas Karamchand Gandhi, *The Essential Gandhi: His Life, Works, and Ideas*, ed. Louis Fischer (New York: Vintage Books, 1962).

77. Lawson and Lafayette, discussion with Wong and Lytle Hernandez.

78. Ibid.

79. Nashville Christian Leadership Council, *Toward the Beloved Community: A Story of the Nashville Christian Leadership Council* (Nashville: NCLC, 1961), crmvet.org, http://www.crmvet.org /docs/61_nclc.pdf. The pamphlet urges Nashville to join the beloved community and "discover ways of non-violent resistance in love to all forms of racial, social, economic, or political injustices" (1).

80. Lawson, "Interview: Rev. James Lawson."

Rev. Martin Luther King Jr. in Montgomery at the end of the bus boycott, December 26, 1956. *Getty Images.*

CHAPTER 2

AWAKENING: THE MONTGOMERY BUS BOYCOTT

Caroline Luce

The story of Montgomery is the story of 50,000 Negroes who were willing to substitute tired feet for tires souls and walk the streets of Montgomery until the walls of segregation were finally battered by the forces of justice.
— Martin Luther King Jr., *Stride toward Freedom*

In early December 1955, while working at Hislop College in Nagpur, India, James M. Lawson Jr. read an article in the local newspaper about a bus boycott that was being staged by African American residents of Montgomery, Alabama. Having studied Mohandas Gandhi's philosophy, Lawson had long thought that nonviolence could be used to contest the morality and legality of segregation in America. The bus boycott confirmed his assessment. "No one in the academic world, the political world, the economic world, ever saw it coming," Lawson said. "It was on the news of the BBC and the All India Radio. . . . It was in Africa, it was in Latin America."[1] What began as a local struggle for better treatment on public buses became an international crusade for justice and equality, uniting clergymen, labor organizers, women's groups, and civil rights organizations into a powerful coalition that brought an end to legal segregation on Montgomery's buses. For 381 days, nearly all of the city's 50,000 black residents stayed off the buses, a powerful display of collective strength that inspired similar boycotts, sit-ins, marches, and freedom rides in local communities across the South.

The Montgomery bus boycott was the first direct-action campaign in the Western world to use the language and tactics of nonviolence to challenge segregation. Its organizers were experienced—they had been fighting for years to improve conditions for African Americans—but they had no model for applying Gandhi's teachings in the Jim Crow South. Instead, they developed their nonviolent strategies through experimentation and practice, stressing the necessity of *being* nonviolent—that is, remaining committed to Christian love and using the "tools of justice"—throughout the campaign.[2] Over the course of the thirteen-month boycott, they forged a new strategy for building and sustaining a grassroots mass movement that activists like Lawson could employ in subsequent campaigns.

SEGREGATION IN MONTGOMERY AND BUILDING A "COALITION OF THE CONSCIOUS"

The Montgomery bus boycott did not erupt spontaneously after the arrest of Rosa Parks. She and other leaders of the boycott had been actively organizing African Americans in Montgomery for decades. In the 1940s they had mobilized a massive voter registration drive throughout the region, offering classes to prepare black Alabamans for the required literacy tests and for staging protests when they were prevented from accessing the registrar. The campaign raised the number of African American voters in Alabama from 250,000 in 1940 to 750,000 by 1948 and helped to secure the election of James Folsom, a populist who advocated equal rights for African Americans, as governor in 1946.[3] African American activists had sought justice for Gertrude Perkins—a young black woman who had been raped by two uniformed police officers—and under the leadership of Parks had formed the Committee for Equal Justice for Recy Taylor, a sharecropper and mother who had been abducted and raped by a group of white men on her way home from church in nearby Abbeville. But none of these efforts had succeeded in garnering the broad-based support necessary to directly challenge the city's segregation laws. Activists needed to focus their efforts on a specific issue so that they could unify the African American community and leverage their collective power to encourage other black residents to take action. African American women testified to the mistreatment and abuse they experienced while riding the city's segregated buses and identified reforming the bus system as a worthy target for a nonviolent campaign. Jo Ann Robinson, a professor of English at Alabama State College, observed that "the bus boycott originated in the demeaning, wretched, intolerable impositions and conditions that black citizens experienced in a caste system commonly called segregation."[4]

The owners of the Montgomery bus line had imposed an elaborate and arbitrary set of rules to maintain segregation on the buses. Even though almost ninety percent of the ridership was African American, the company required that ten seats be left empty for white passengers even when the rest of the bus was full. African American riders were also required to exit the bus after paying their fare and re-enter through the back doors to avoid walking through the white section. When a white passenger could not find a seat, African American passengers were required to vacate not only their seats but also the flanking row, so that the black passengers were always seated behind the white ones. African American women, who constituted a majority of the bus riders, found the seating policies particularly exasperating because they often carried children, groceries, or packages. Enforcement of

Because in a very real way, **in the heart of it**, . . . [the Montgomery Bus Boycott] was a major movement **challenging the social oppression** and social tyrannies. No such national cleansing had ever occurred before. **It was the beginning of the nonviolent dimension**, the nonviolent action dimension, of the civil rights movement.
　　—Rev. Lawson April 2013

Rosa Parks, with Rev. Martin Luther King Jr. in the background, ca. 1955.

the rules was left entirely in the hands of the white bus drivers, allowing them to impose segregation on the buses at their discretion. Their enforcement involved vicious insults and physical abuse, and they could eject passengers from the bus no matter how far they were from their destination. This mistreatment of African American women was a daily reminder of their status, as Parks has described: "Our existence was for the white man's comfort and well being; we had to accept being deprived of just being human."[5]

The busing policies were one element of a comprehensive system of segregation that had prevailed in Alabama and throughout the South since the late nineteenth century. African American Alabamans made great strides toward equality in the decades after the Civil War, but beginning in the 1880s white supremacist legislators, eager to "redeem" the South's former glory, began to roll back the civil rights protections afforded to African Americans by the Fourteenth and Fifteenth Amendments. By 1901 Alabama state legislators had amended the state's constitution to include poll taxes, literacy tests, and other restrictive voting requirements that effectively stripped the black community of its growing political power; while some 180,000 black Alabamans had been registered to vote in 1900, just two years later only 3,000 were on the rolls.[6] Having weakened the power of the African American vote, state and local politicians then moved to pass laws and ordinances that enforced the strict separation of the races. These efforts were boosted when the US Supreme Court upheld the right of states to maintain "separate but equal" public facilities for African Americans in its decision in *Plessy v. Ferguson*. The segregation laws applied to both private and public spaces and regimented interracial encounters in virtually every aspect of life, often to the point of absurdity. For example, Alabama law not only prevented African Americans and whites from eating together but also mandated that businesses serving food erect seven-foot partitions between black and white diners as well as furnish separate entrances and bathrooms. Laws establishing curfews and limiting African American access to parks and other public spaces greatly reduced their mobility, and contract-enforcement statutes and vagrancy laws made it very difficult for African American workers to challenge the fairness of their contracts and exit from agreements with abusive employers, facilitating the continued exploitation of black labor. Through intricate legislative and legal maneuvers, city and state officials preserved white supremacy in Montgomery and throughout the South.

Those who transgressed the racial boundaries imposed by the segregation laws faced tremendous, sometimes fatal, consequences when local white supremacists and vigilante groups took it upon themselves to enforce the separation of the races. In total, some 4,742 African Americans in the South died at the hands of lynch mobs between 1882 and 1968, including 262 Alabamans between 1882 and 1930.[7] Many who were falsely accused of crimes or of having violated "proper" racial etiquette were abducted by mobs, their bodies later found mutilated, dismembered, and burned. Even African Americans prosecuted through Alabama courts faced violent punishments because nearly all the state's lawyers, judges, and juries were white. African American defendants were far more likely than whites to incur stiff sentences and capital punishment. Convict-leasing laws allowed local governments to bond out prisoners to private businesses that included lumber, mining, and railroad companies, and incarceration often resulted in brutal forced labor in chain gangs. Although African American women were less likely than men to be lynched or incarcerated, they faced a tremendous amount of sexual violence, including attacks from their employers, rape, and harassment on streetcars and sidewalks and in parks and other public spaces. Like lynching, rape and other forms of violence in the segregated South served as "tools of psychological and physical intimidation" that reinforced white supremacy by stripping black bodies of their humanity and underscoring the cheapness of black life.[8]

Through disenfranchisement and other legal maneuvers, along with state-sanctioned and extralegal violence, white supremacists in the South created a system of segregation that, as Lawson described, not only deprived African Americans of the "fundamental necessities of life and their fundamental rights" but also their "fundamental dignity and humanity."[9] Segregation impacted the life of every African American who lived in Montgomery, and even those who had not been victimized themselves knew a family member, fellow church-goer, or friend who had been. Indeed, the structural inequalities of segregation were built into the geography of the city itself. Montgomery had been home to a prosperous community of African Americans since the days of Reconstruction. These residents included the middle-class professionals and small business owners who had been educated at Alabama State College and had settled in the affluent black neighborhood on Centennial Hill. The demographics of the city began to change in the 1920s as the decline of the cotton economy brought thousands of displaced African American farmers and sharecroppers to the city. They sought jobs in Montgomery's lumber and textile mills, metal shops, fertilizer plants, and nearby airfields, causing housing shortages and overcrowding in the other, lower income areas of town where blacks were permitted live. As the number of African American residents surpassed 50,000, city services struggled to keep pace with Montgomery's growing population. In 1948 there was only one public high school open to African American students. In the poorest black neighborhoods, like "Bogge Homa," which had once been a camp for cotton drivers, over 70 percent of residences did not have running water or flush toilets.[10] The squalor in these neighborhoods was a physical embodiment of the massive disparities of wealth and power that segregation had created.

Political cartoon by Laura Gray commenting on the Montgomery bus boycott. It appeared in the *Militant* on February 13, 1956. *Courtesy Marxists Internet Archive.*

Montgomery's racially stratified geography forced most of the African American population to rely on city buses to get around town. Nearly two-thirds of African American women in Montgomery worked as "day ladies"—domestics, cooks, and housekeepers—who often worked shifts of over ten hours for wages as low as two dollars a day.[11] They served in the homes of white families, most of whom lived in the affluent districts in the southern and eastern part of town. This required African American working women to travel great distances to and from their jobs every day. African American men who worked as unskilled laborers, as "yard boys," or in the service sector of the downtown commercial district also traversed the city for work. So too did African American students, many of whom had to take the bus to their schools across town.[12] Many middle-class African American families owned cars, which proved crucial to the success of the boycott, but wives were often forced to ride the bus while their husbands were at work. As a result, nearly every African American resident of Montgomery depended on the buses, regardless of their income level or profession. And in turn, nearly every African American resident had either been mistreated on the buses or had born witness to the abuse of other black riders. For example, Robinson remembered clearly the "waves of humiliation" she felt after a driver shoved her off the bus when she accidentally sat in the white section in 1949.[13] A year later, a young black veteran named Thomas Edward Brooks was beaten, shot, and killed by a police officer near downtown Montgomery after he got into an argument with a bus driver who refused to refund his fare. The buses were such a frequent site of abuse that many African Americans in Montgomery referred to them as "yellow monsters."[14]

A society that displays colored signs **encourages white people to be hostile**, to be ugly. **Hostility against black** people was a natural part of segregated society.
—Rev. Lawson April 2013

Several years before the bus boycott began, the Women's Political Council (WPC), a group led by Robinson and composed of educators, social workers, nurses, and other African American professionals, began organizing the women of Centennial Hill to fight mistreatment on the yellow monsters. The WPC had been established to address a broad range of issues in the African American community, including "juvenile and adult delinquency" and voter registration, but after receiving dozens of complaints from black riders, it began concentrating its efforts on improving conditions on the buses. Robinson recalled that in the months before Parks's arrest, some thirty women had come to the WPC to report mistreatment by bus drivers, including Mrs. Epsie Worthy, who described being harassed and beaten by a driver and then being arrested by the police when she tried to defend herself.[15] As they heard the complaints, the members of the WPC began to see their individual feelings of shame and embarrassment as a collective experience and to understand that the abuse they suffered on the buses was the result not of personal failings but rather of an institutional practice in dire need of reform. They began petitioning the city commissioners to demand changes in the bus company's policies, and they won small concessions from the mayor in 1952 after they offered accounts at a commission meeting of the abuse they had experienced. These African American women refused to hide their pain, using their experiences as weapons in their fight for bus reform.[16]

Beginning in May 1954, immediately after the US Supreme Court declared that "separate educational facilities are inherently unequal" in *Brown v. Board of Education,* the WPC expanded its reform efforts and began threatening to boycott the buses if their demands were not met. Robinson knew that the bus company relied on African American dollars to survive, giving the black community economic leverage in a system in which they were otherwise marginalized or excluded. She also knew that a boycott would generate broad support in the African American community because of the litany of complaints that could be leveled against the bus company, but that it would take a precipitating event for the black community to come together. When a fifteen-year-old African American student named Claudette Colvin was arrested for refusing to give up her seat on a bus in March 1955, Robinson and the WPC saw their opportunity.

Colvin was a junior at Booker T. Washington High School, and she rode the bus every day from her home in King Hill on the north side to attend school in the center of the city. A quiet and devoted student, Colvin had grown increasingly frustrated with the injustices faced by African Americans in Montgomery after Jeremiah Reeves, a popular senior from her school, was arrested and sentenced to death for raping a white housewife, a charge to which he confessed but subsequently denied. Along with other students, she attended rallies, raised funds for Reeves's legal defense, and joined the youth council of the National Association for the Advancement of Colored People (NAACP), which was directed by Parks.

On her way home from school on March 2, Colvin was ordered to move from her seat after a white couple sat in the colored section. She refused. The bus driver called the police. After Colvin told the officers that she would not move because she was "just as good as any white person," they dragged her off of the bus, kicking and screaming. The officers arrested her, charging her not only with violating a state segregation ordinance but also with disturbing the peace and assaulting a police officer.[17] News of the arrest rippled through the African American community, and the WPC announced that they were prepared to mount a boycott of the buses in response.

Unfortunately, many of the city's other African American leaders refused to act in support of Colvin, and her case failed to generate the community-wide support the WPC desired. Although every black Alabaman recognized the evils of segregation, the overwhelming threat of violence and recrimination made many reluctant or fearful to act. In the eyes of Martin Luther King Jr., that reluctance was also the product of the "appalling lack of unity" among the leaders of the city's sixty-eight black organizations. According to King, those leaders were "at loggerheads with one another" when he arrived in Montgomery in the fall of 1954, divided by personal conflicts, class-based tensions, and disagreements about how best to bring an end to segregation.[18] Many affluent African Americans from Centennial Hill believed that ensuring equality required removing all barriers of racial discrimination, both collectively, through the democratic process and the courts, and personally, through self-improvement and education. Most maintained high standards of respectability that were based on traditional values of temperance, etiquette, and hard work, and they were often quick to fault the behavior of poor African Americans.[19]

Others, including E. D. Nixon of the Brotherhood of Sleeping Car Porters (BSCP), believed more aggressive action was needed to improve the lives of the poor, and they called for a grassroots community mobilization rather than cooperation with city officials and gradual reform. Nixon, who was inspired by the BSCP's founder, A. Philip Randolph, blamed the injustices of capitalism for the poverty and violence faced by working-class African Americans and was sometimes critical of the more affluent community leaders.[20] Nixon and the middle-class leaders of Centennial Hill condemned the city's conservative African American ministers for their unwillingness to address the issue of segregation and for refusing to get their congregations more involved in the struggle for civil rights. The "indifference," "apathy," and "crippling factionalism" that King observed among these leaders and their organizations led him to conclude that "no lasting social reform could ever be achieved in Montgomery."[21]

Colvin's arrest exacerbated these tensions. Despite the widespread outcry among African American residents, some local black leaders argued that Colvin's "feisty" behavior was to blame for her mistreatment. Rumors began to fly about her upbringing in King Hill (widely regarded as a "depressed and dangerous" neighborhood), the character of her parents (a "day lady" and a "yard boy"), and her "rebellious" ways, prompting some leaders, including Parks, to conclude that Colvin had "stepped outside the bounds of respectable behavior" for a black woman.[22] Complicating matters further, in the months that followed her arrest, Colvin revealed that she was pregnant to an unnamed father and dropped out of school. Even Nixon, a consistent advocate on behalf of the African American working class, decided that Colvin was "unfit" to be the face of a long-term protest campaign.[23] Colvin was found guilty at her trial, and the WPC backed away from their boycott plans.

Even though Colvin's arrest failed to inspire a unified, community-wide response, it did serve as a crucial first step toward a boycott. The widespread outrage over Colvin's arrest showed that reforming the buses could be a specific issue through which the African American community could fight the injustices of segregation more broadly. As a result,

African American leaders began to consolidate a coalition around that specific target. Representatives from dozens of black organizations formed a coordinating committee, which was chaired by wealthy African American entrepreneur Rufus Lewis, to work with city officials for reform. African American church leaders, many of whom had to that point been reluctant to get involved, formed the Interdenominational Ministerial Alliance as a vehicle for coordinating their efforts.[24] Over the summer and fall months of 1955, these groups began meeting together to discuss plans for a boycott and to develop strategies for sustaining an enduring challenge to segregation in Montgomery.

On December 1, amidst these ongoing discussions, Parks was arrested when she refused to give up her seat on the bus. A devout churchgoer and an active leader in the local NAACP, she was "respected in all black circles" in Montgomery and news of her arrest "traveled like wildfire."[25] Even though their plans had not been finalized, the city's African American leaders knew instantly that it was time to act. That night Robinson and other WPC members printed more than 52,000 flyers and papered African American homes, cars, schools, and businesses before sunrise. The flyers framed their calls for a boycott on gendered terms.

> Another Negro Woman has been arrested and thrown in jail because she refused to give up her seat on the bus for a white person to sit down. . . . Negroes have rights, too, for if Negroes did not ride the buses, they could not operate. Three-fourths of the riders are Negroes, yet we are arrested, or have to stand over empty seats. If we do not do something to stop these arrests, they will continue. Next time it may be you, or your daughter, or your mother. . . . We are, therefore, asking every Negro to stay off the buses Monday in protest of the arrest and trial. Don't ride the buses to work, to town, to school or anywhere on Monday.[26]

More flyers were distributed over the weekend, calling on boycotters to attend a rally at the courthouse and a mass meeting afterward at Holt Street Baptist Church. Those who owned cars were encouraged to carpool, and the city's African American taxi drivers showed their support by agreeing to offer discounted rides to boycotters. Nixon persuaded the ministers of the Interdenominational Ministerial Alliance to do their part during Sunday services by calling on their congregations to join the boycott. When Monday morning came, the results were spectacular: with only a very few exceptions, no African American riders boarded the buses.

PREPARING FOR DIRECT ACTION

The leaders of the boycott had organized the mass meeting at Holt Street Baptist Church to serve as a closing ceremony for their one-day protest, where they could calm emotions and address any issues that emerged. Representatives of the city's African American organizations agreed to meet beforehand to evaluate their efforts, but the boycott's success had so vastly exceeded expectations that the gathering became an emergency planning and strategy session. Most of the leaders agreed that the boycott should be continued, but they recognized that they needed to define a clear set of demands and a plan for action if they were to rally the community's support at the mass meeting. The church was quickly filling up with jubilant boycotters, so decisions had to be made fast.

By all accounts, the discussion was intense and at times heated. Those in attendance argued over the potential risks of the boycott, the repercussions boycotters might face, and what level of reform they could possibly expect. They decided that the best way to avoid inflaming existing personal and organizational rivalries was to form an entirely new organization to direct the boycott, the Montgomery Improvement Association (MIA). They selected a relative newcomer, the young King, as president. They also elected seven officers, including Nixon, and a thirty-five-person executive board that included many of the city's African American ministers as well as Robinson and several other WPC members. Rather than call for full integration of the buses, they agreed to a more moderate set of demands that were based on the reforms the WPC had been pursuing for months: more courteous treatment by bus drivers, increased employment of African American bus drivers, and first come, first served seating, so that no African American passenger could be asked to move. They then presented their plans to the crowd, which had grown to 6,000 inside the building and hundreds more on the street outside, asking them to vote on a resolution to continue the boycott until the bus company and the city met their demands.

All the speeches at the meeting stressed that the boycott would require personal sacrifice, discipline, and perseverance. Nixon and others warned the crowd that the boycott would be "a long, drawn-out affair."[27] But each speaker also reminded the attendees that they had already sacrificed and persevered for years just to survive. King, for example, praised the "amazing patience" that the African American community had shown and used the crowd's shared experiences to issue a call for collective action.

> There comes a time when people get tired of being trampled over by the feet of oppression. There comes a time, my friends, when people get tired of being plunged across the abyss of humiliation, where they experience the bleakness of hugging despair. There comes a time when people get tired of being pushed out of the glittering sunlight of life's July and left standing amid the piercing chill of alpine November. . . . We are here tonight to be saved from the patience that makes us patient with anything less than freedom and justice.[28]

In the soaring rhetoric that would become his signature style, King encouraged the audience to see their suffering as a source of strength rather than a cause for hopelessness. He framed the sacrifice required of the boycotters as a way to fight back against the pain and embarrassment they had endured for so long, thereby "transforming bitter memories and shame into weapons of protest."[29] His speech reframed suffering and sacrifice as motivating calls to action and converted a sense of collective injustice into a basis for collective power.

The speeches, particularly those by the ministers, embraced a higher moral purpose for the bus boycott and articulated values that would drive the movement. The ministers based their pleas for lawfulness, peace, and self-control on biblical teachings and appealed to the largely churchgoing crowd to follow in the footsteps of Jesus. King linked being nonviolent and fighting for justice to faith and religious expression.

> There will be no crosses burned at any bus stops in Montgomery. There will be no white persons pulled out of their homes and taken out on some distant road and lynched for not cooperating. . . . I want to stress this, in all of our doings, in all of our deliberations here in this evening and all of the week and while—whatever we do, we must keep God in the forefront. Let us be Christian in all of our actions. But I want to tell you this evening that it is not enough for us to talk about love, love is one of the pivotal points of the Christian faith. There is another side called justice. And justice is really love in calculation. Justice is love correcting that which revolts against love. . . . Standing beside love is always justice, and we are only using the tools of justice.[30]

Like Gandhi, King recognized love as a powerful weapon that, when demonstrated collectively, could alter the public consciousness. The notion of justice as "love in calculation" that King advanced at Holt Street Baptist Church bore a noticeable resemblance to Gandhi's concept of agape, or "love in action."[31] In the earliest days of the campaign, however, King avoided the language of nonviolence and instead drew from the scriptures to persuade the boycotters of the righteousness of the movement. In his memoir, *Stride toward Freedom*, he described the ethos of the movement as "the Christian doctrine of love operating through the Gandhian method of nonviolence. . . . Christ furnished the spirit and motivation, while Gandhi furnished the method."[32] King and other MIA leaders affirmed the nonviolent, Christian ethos of their campaign in speeches made at the first mass meeting and hundreds of other events thereafter, giving the activities of the boycotters moral sanction and bolstering their spiritual conviction. By the end of the meeting, nearly the entire crowd was on its feet. Participants voted unanimously to stay off the buses until the bus company and the city met the MIA's demands. In the course of a few hours, King and the other leaders of the MIA had used the success of a one-day boycott to build the foundation for a lasting campaign against segregation. They had clearly defined their shared goals, issued an ultimatum to their opponents, and outlined a basic set of tactics that they would use in the campaign—what King referred to as "the tools of justice."

DIRECT ACTION AND NONVIOLENT TACTICS IN MONTGOMERY

Although their first meeting had been rushed, the founders of the MIA had decades of organizing experience and came to the meeting prepared with strong ideas about how to conduct the campaign. The WPC had been developing a plan for carrying out a long-term bus boycott for months, and the leaders of the local NAACP had been eagerly awaiting an opportunity to contest segregation in the courts. Church leaders offered their resources and ideas for mobilizing their congregations. Together they agreed on three goals that would guide the campaign: forming a transportation committee to provide rides to boycotters, scheduling weekly meetings to coordinate activities and boost morale, and raising funds for a legal battle to appeal Parks's conviction. Each fit within the Christian ethos of the boycott put forth by the speakers at Holt Street Baptist Church, and each proved lasting and effective. Local white supremacists, together with Montgomery's city leaders and others who sought to maintain segregation, developed their own tactics to stifle and suppress the MIA's activities, often relying on violent means to achieve their goal of ending the boycott. The MIA had to create new tactics in response to the violent backlash, and increasingly they borrowed from Gandhi's teachings and practices, gradually introducing the language and philosophy of nonviolence into the campaign.

Perhaps the most crucial tactic employed in Montgomery was the implementation of the MIA's transportation system, developed to address the practical challenges of ensuring that tens of thousands of African American workers could get to their jobs without riding the bus. At first the transportation committee, led by Robinson and Lewis, relied heavily on the city's African American taxi drivers, but local officials soon prohibited the taxi drivers from offering discounted fares and the committee had to develop an elaborate system of carpools. They created a map with forty-two pick-up stations at African American–owned stores, club houses, churches, and homes and devised a dispatch service, staffed largely by members of the WPC, which sent dozens of cars out to locations across the city in the mornings and late afternoons. African American and white residents volunteered their own cars for carpools, and local churches purchased large vans to shuttle their congregants. The transportation committee eventually managed a fleet of over three hundred cars. At the two largest pick-up stations downtown—an African American–owned parking lot and a nearby drugstore—carpoolers could transfer to different neighborhood lines or hitch a ride from a car passing through. As the costs of offering the rides began to add up, churches took up collections for gas money to give to volunteer drivers, and when donations began pouring in from across the country, the MIA hired a dozen drivers and purchased two of their own "people's" gas stations.[33]

Other boycotters simply walked, traveling up to fifteen to twenty miles a day between their workplaces and the segregated districts in which they lived. Most African American bus riders had walked the routes at some point as a consequence of either being kicked off the bus or getting off to avoid a more violent confrontation. During the boycott, walking became a collective act of protest and an expression of dignity, self-respect, and power. One minister recalled that when he offered an older woman a ride, she told him she did not mind walking because "my body may be a bit tired, but for many years now my soul has been tired. Now my soul is resting. So I don't mind if my body is tired, because my soul is free."[34] Working women also built strong friendships and support networks and reinforced one another's determination by walking together. So many African American residents chose to walk that the MIA and local African American churches began collecting and purchasing new shoes to give to those whose soles had worn through. The "walking contingent" and the carpool program together created an alternative system of transportation that allowed nearly every one of Montgomery's 50,000 African American residents to avoid the buses for 381 days.[35]

The MIA's extensive schedule of social events also provided vital infrastructure for the campaign by cultivating a powerful sense of community among the boycotters. At first the meetings were held on Monday nights at various churches in Centennial Hill. Later the MIA added a second meeting on Thursday nights, held in churches in lower-income neighborhoods on the west side of town. People often showed up hours early to secure their seat, passing the time by reading, chatting, and singing together. Speakers reported news, reinforced the biblical teachings guiding the movement, stressed the necessity of remaining peaceful, and offered weekly pep talks to the boycotters.[36] Each meeting also included testimonials from boycotters about their reasons for joining the boycott, their experiences of abuse, and their stories of courage and defiance. Echoing the WPC's strategy in their fight for bus reform, the weekly meetings provided important opportunities for African American women to assert their rights by testifying to their painful experiences and to be recognized and celebrated for their sacrifices, which strengthened their commitment to the boycott campaign.

Other social events were organized and publicized through the MIA's two most important communication networks: the churches and the WPC, which expanded to branches in three neighborhoods throughout the city. Through these networks the MIA promoted dozens of dances, parties, and picnics, where attendees got together to raise money and celebrate their unity. The events gave African American women opportunities to fill leadership roles in the campaign and to use their culinary talents—which their white employers took for granted—as fundraising tools.[37] And, perhaps most important, these functions were occasions for the boycotters to socialize and get to know one another. Robinson relates that maids mingled with black elites at MIA events, and "PhDs and no ds got together" to sing, pray, and share stories, fostering a unity that transcended the class tensions within the black community.[38]

Another tactic, which was implemented in the first days of the boycott, was to fight bus segregation in the courts. The legal challenge was directed by two young African American attorneys, Fred Gray and Charles Langford, with the help of Clifford Durr. Although initially deemed the "perfect plaintiff," the circumstances of Parks's arrest and the resulting boycott made it likely that her conviction would be thrown out and the opportunity to challenge the constitutionality of the city's segregation ordinance would be lost.[39] Instead, Gray and Langford decided to bundle several cases together. They resurrected Colvin's case

There were black people in Montgomery **who just never took a bus** because of the horrid treatment they could expect. **So they walked** even if it meant walking ten, fifteen, twenty, thirty miles a day, **they would walk**. They would **never take the bus**.
  —Rev. Lawson April 2013

and those of Mary Louise Smith, Susie McDonald, and Aurelia S. Browder and used their convictions as grounds for suing the city, Mayor William A. Gayle, and the bus company for violating their rights to equal protection under the Fourteenth Amendment. The lawsuit was filed on February 1, 1956, three months after Parks was arrested.[40]

While the case, *Browder v. Gayle*, slowly worked its way through the courts, Nixon, King, and other prominent leaders traveled around the country, raising money for the legal fund. Nixon spread the word about what was happening in Montgomery to union locals, which raised funds for the MIA from their members. The United Auto Workers in Detroit alone donated thirty-five thousand dollars.[41] Robinson began publishing the *MIA* Newsletter to keep their supporters outside of Montgomery informed about developments in the campaign. King served as the public spokesperson for the boycott, giving impassioned appeals and explanations of the MIA's goals to local and national radio and television reporters. The legal campaign served as an organizing tool, helping the MIA to build regional, national, and international solidarity networks and making the Montgomery bus boycott one of the most widely know protest movements in the world.

Unfortunately, the boycott's endurance and increasing renown prompted a racial backlash in Montgomery. The bus company had been forced to cancel eight of its lines and lay off almost forty drivers, and its owner, along with downtown business owners whose Christmas sales had been hurt by the absence of black shoppers, began pressuring city leaders to intervene. In mid-January the mayor announced a new "get tough" policy on the boycott, and local police officers began issuing tickets to boycotters for loitering and hitchhiking and to carpool drivers for scurrilous moving violations. The police harassment was coupled with an informal "hate campaign," mostly by white teenagers who threw water balloons and rotten eggs, potatoes, and apples from cars and made menacing prank phone calls to organizers. By the end of the month the "hate campaign" had reached new levels of violence: a bomb exploded on the doorstep of King's home in Centennial Hill while his wife and child were inside. The following evening another bomb exploded at Nixon's house. A few days later, ten thousand white supremacists descended on the city to attend a pro-segregation "White Citizens Convocation" organized at the Montgomery Coliseum. It featured remarks by Clyde C. Sellers, the police commissioner, and a keynote address by James O.

Eastland, US senator from Mississippi.[42] During the cold months of winter, the city issued injunctions against the carpoolers to prevent them from offering rides, which forced even more boycotters to walk through the rain and mud and heightened racial tensions on the streets of Montgomery.

King's commitment to nonviolence was enormously important in those dark days of winter, particularly after his home was bombed. Although no one was hurt, the brazen attack stirred anger and outrage, and within hours a large, angry crowd had gathered outside his home. King calmed the crowd, saying,

> We cannot solve this problem through retaliatory violence. We must meet violence with nonviolence. Remember the words of Jesus: "He who lives by the sword will perish by the sword." . . . We must love our white brothers . . . no matter what they do to us. We must make them know that we love them. Jesus still cries out in words that echo across the centuries: "Love your enemies; bless them that curse you; pray for them that despitefully use you." This is what we must live by. We must meet hate with love.[43]

King's resilience and unwillingness to arm himself after the bombing impressed even his closest confidants, including Rev. Ralph Abernathy, his friend and the vice president of MIA, who insisted that he hire a bodyguard and post armed guards at his home. King refused, but members of his church soon formed a voluntary security team to protect him and his family.

Ultimately, it was the commitment to nonviolence shown by the boycotters themselves that ensured the movement's success. African Americans who walked to work and school became the primary targets of white retaliation. They were taunted by onlookers and police, who attempted to goad them into violence and pressure them to ride the buses again. Although they had not received training in passive resistance, the boycotters remained peaceful and nonviolent through all thirteen months of the boycott. The movement transformed their anger into courage and resolve, as one woman noted at a mass meeting: "I am filled up to my bones . . . it's way down in my bones and when there ain't no protest, I'm still gonna have it. I'm still gonna have my protest."[44] Speeches made by King and other ministers served to encourage and embolden the boycotters, but it was through practicing nonviolence on a daily basis that their experiences of injustice and abuse became sources of individual and collective empowerment.

Dissatisfied by the results of his "get tough" policy, the mayor then moved to use the law to shut down the boycott entirely. He and his allies dug up an antiboycott ordinance passed in 1903 after a streetcar boycott organized by local African America ministers first challenged the segregation of public transportation. The incredibly restrictive law prohibited any "boycotting . . . picketing or other interference with . . . lawful business" as well as "publishing or declaring that a boycott . . . exists or has existed," thereby criminalizing boycotts as well as any effort on the part of individuals or the press to discuss, promote, or circulate information about boycotts.[45] Local law enforcement officials used the law to justify the mass arrests of virtually every prominent African American in Montgomery, including Parks, King, Nixon, Robinson, and dozens of local ministers. In total, 115 boycotters were indicted. The judge issued a three-hundred-dollar bond for each, a blow that threatened to devastate the finances of the MIA.

The mass arrests began on February 22, and King and other ministers were detained first. Quickly the protesters, under the advice of Bayard Rustin of the Fellowship of Reconciliation (FOR), who had come to Montgomery to lend his experience to the boycott, traveled to the police station together to turn themselves in. To the great surprise of the local police

Rosa Parks and King came to represent, nonviolent struggle. **There was a deep sensibility among black people** that Jim Crow law and segregation was **absolutely wrong**.

—Rev. Lawson April 2013

force, over eighty men and women for whom they had issued arrest warrants appeared in the police station voluntarily to be photographed, fingerprinted, and taken into custody, creating a relaxed, even jolly, atmosphere in the booking room. Robinson remembers people chatting, joking around, and laughing with the officers while they were being arrested, until one policeman got so angry that he pushed her down the hall to the bondsman to be released.[46]

For decades the police in Montgomery and throughout the South had wielded their power to arrest and incarcerate African Americans as a means of enforcing white supremacy, using fear to intimidate and suppress those who challenged segregation. By appearing at the station voluntarily and showing no fear as they were being arrested, the boycotters took that power away from the police. They created an atmosphere of calm, peaceful solidarity in what had been a site of terror, abuse, and violence, engendering what Robinson described as a "helpless anger" in some of the officers.[47] Rather than cripple the boycott as intended, the mass arrests served to demonstrate the boycotters' strength. The next morning the *New York Times* published the now iconic photo of Parks that was taken during the mass arrests, igniting an international media firestorm. The arrests inspired sympathy boycotts of segregated bus lines in black communities as far away as Capetown, South Africa, and the national conversation about what was happening in Montgomery grew so loud that President Dwight D Eisenhower was questioned about it in press conferences. By the time the trial began in March, the media had descended on Montgomery, providing the MIA with an unprecedented opportunity to air their grievances against segregation. Thirty-one witnesses testified to the abuse they had experienced on the buses. Twenty-seven of them were women, including Stella Brooks, wife of the African American veteran who had been killed by police in 1950 after arguing with a bus driver.

Despite his repeated insistence that he had "urged nonviolence at all points," King was convicted along with Nixon and two other activists and fined five hundred dollars for having conspired to break the boycott law through violence and coercion.[48] Later, King would explain that his problem with the conviction was that it misrepresented the goals of the campaign: "Our aim has never been to put the bus company out of business, but rather to put justice in business."[49]

In the wake of the mass arrests, the leaders of the MIA developed a new direct-action tactic for the first day of King's trial. The boycotters would first march to the courthouse for the trial and then march back to Dexter Avenue Baptist Church for a prayer meeting. At a mass meeting held on the evening of the arrests, Abernathy asked those in attendance not

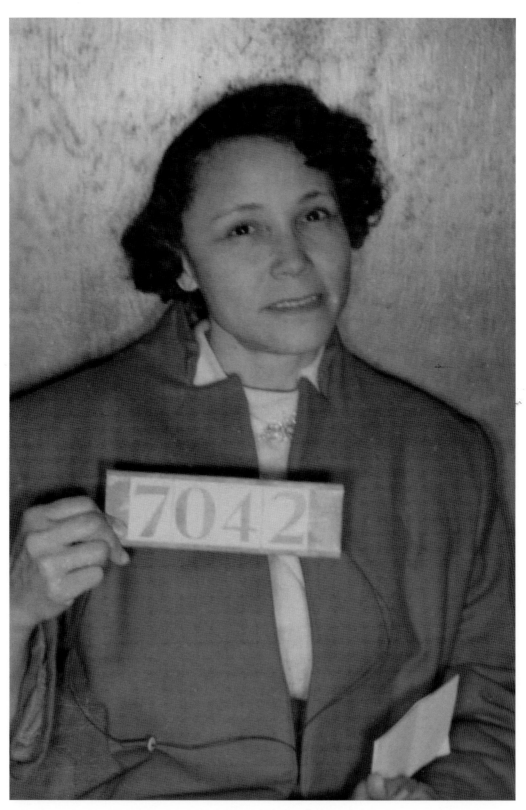

Booking photograph of Jo Ann Robinson, taken on February 21, 1956, when she was arrested for participating in the Montgomery bus boycott. *Courtesy of the Montgomery County Alabama Archives.*

to use their cars, and he suspended the carpool program. For that one day, Pilgrim-Prayer Day, every boycotter would be on foot, "so that those who walked would know that others walked with them."[50] The event was inspired by the actions of Jesus, who carried the cross to his crucifixion, and Gandhi, who walked 240 miles with thousands of Indians to protest the British salt tax, elegantly blending Christian ethos and Gandhian methods.[51] In drizzling rain, thousands marched in silence, in prayer, and in song, fortifying their unity during the darkest days of the boycott.

The mass arrests and the trial also brought reinforcements to Montgomery: experienced activists in the national struggle for civil rights who were deeply committed to and well versed in Gandhi's teachings on nonviolence. Rustin had come first, but was forced to leave after a newspaper editor threatened to out him as a homosexual. Rev. Glenn Smiley and others affiliated with FOR came to take his place.[52] Smiley helped organize trainings and workshops through which boycotters learned to express themselves in the language of nonviolence and to engage in civil disobedience, deepening Gandhi's influence on the boycott movement. He also personally counseled King and became his mentor on the philosophy and tactics of nonviolence. Rustin's and Smiley's time in Montgomery introduced new "tools of justice" into the campaign and provided an infusion of energy to sustain the boycott into the spring.

In June, more than six months after Parks's arrest, the MIA won its first legal victory when a panel of three US district court judges declared the segregation of Montgomery's buses to be unconstitutional in *Browder v. Gayle*. Recognizing that the ruling would be appealed, the leaders of the MIA curtailed their celebration and vowed to continue the boycott. The US Supreme Court agreed to hear the case, and hearings were scheduled for the

Paintings by Charlotta Janssen of the booking photographs taken when Martin Luther King Jr. and Rosa Parks were arrested for their participation in the Montgomery bus boycott. *Courtesy of Charlotta Janssen.*

fall. But the lower court victory provided a boost for the weary boycotters and strengthened their conviction that their sacrifices would not be in vain.

More bombs exploded in Montgomery during the summer months, but as fall approached, the leaders of the MIA could sense that the end of their fight was near. On November 15, 1956, the Court upheld the district court's decision, ending the legal segregation of Montgomery's bus lines. The city and state both quickly filed petitions for reconsideration, and 5,000 Ku Klux Klan members descended on Montgomery, vowing to resist the Court's decision and enforce segregation themselves. The leaders of the MIA, however, set their sights on the future.

In December 1956, in honor of the anniversary of the start of the boycott, Montgomery hosted a weeklong celebration called the "Institute on Non-Violence and Social Change." The event included prayer meetings, training sessions, and workshops on voter registration and nonviolent resistance. King gave a speech in which he reflected on what had been accomplished during the boycott.

> We have gained a new sense of dignity and destiny. We have discovered a new and powerful weapon—nonviolent resistance. . . . This dynamic unity, this amazing self-respect, this willingness to suffer, this refusal to hit back will soon cause the oppressor to becomeashamed of his own methods.[53]

The event organizers drew on the network that they had formed over the course of the boycott, assembling veteran and younger activists from throughout the region, who shared their ideas and experiences. Together they created an exportable model for building and sustaining a direct-action campaign that was based on the boycott and foregrounded the philosophy and tactics of nonviolence. Activists employed this model in local struggles throughout the South in the 1950s and 1960s, and others continue to use it to fight for social justice to this day.

Less than two weeks later, on December 20, the US Supreme Court rejected the petitions that had been filed by the city and state and issued a court order to integrate the buses. The MIA declared the victorious end of their boycott. The next morning Nixon boarded an integrated bus near his house in Peacock Tract with Abernathy, Smiley, and King. Nixon had spent the morning crying. Overcome with emotion, he worried that he might erupt in tears again. But then his old friend Parks climbed on board and he found that he no longer felt like crying.

> Her eyes caught mine, and we knew what we'd done, and we both grinned real big and didn't say nothing. We just rode. It was the best ride I ever had in my life, just riding through downtown and out to the west and back again, going nowhere but feeling like we was headed to heaven.[54]

LEGACIES OF THE MONTGOMERY BUS BOYCOTT

Lawson has pointed out that the nonviolence employed in Montgomery resulted in not only a personal but also a collective transformation for all involved. Practicing nonviolence, Lawson noted, requires tremendous sacrifice, self-control, and discipline, which allows an individual to channel his or her anger and fear into strength based on love. Like Lawson, King grounded his teachings on nonviolence in deep religious traditions of the African American church, giving the movement a humanitarian purpose and moral sanction that made participants feel that they were part of something bigger than themselves. By riding in carpools, donating the their time and money, and walking to work, the men and women who had been deprived of their humanity under segregation came to recognize their own

Rosa Parks sits near the front of a bus in Montgomery after the end of the boycott, December 21, 1956. *Courtesy of Corbis Images.*

Rev. Glenn Smiley and Rev. Martin Luther King Jr. ride on a newly integrated bus in Montgomery, December 21, 1956. *Courtesy of Corbis Images.*

power—their "capacity to achieve purpose" and to affect positive social change.[55] Parks described the awakening she experienced in the moment before her arrest.

> I felt a determination cover my body like a quilt on a winter night. I felt all the meanness of every white driver I'd seen who'd been ugly to me and other black people through the years I'd know on the buses in Montgomery. I felt a light suddenly shine through the darkness.[56]

Once Parks felt that light shine, it could never be extinguished. She paid a price for her involvement in the boycott: she was forced to leave Montgomery in 1957 because she and her husband could not find work. They settled in Detroit, where she continued her work with young African Americans. Her commitment to improving her community and fighting for justice endured until the end of her life.

Individual empowerment, when multiplied by thousands, became what Lawson has described as "a power that cannot be stopped, vanquished, . . . manipulated or managed . . . the power of people united around a common purpose."[57] The endurance of the bus boycott and the resolve of the participants surprised even the most devoted activists, prompting them to reconsider what was possible in the black struggle for freedom. Within a month of the boycott's conclusion, King and Abernathy worked with Rustin, Ella Baker, and other veteran activists to form a new regional organization they called the Southern Leadership Conference on Transportation and Nonviolent Integration (later the Southern Christian Leadership Conference). The purpose was to advance a new style of community mobilization based on the philosophy, language, and tactics of nonviolence.

The boycott also inspired a generation of younger African Americans to become more involved in the struggle. One was Lawson, who had returned to the United States from India in 1955. These young activists learned from older, veteran leaders and organized a wave of sit-ins, boycotts, marches, and other forms of nonviolent activism in Selma, Birmingham, Tallahassee, Greensboro, and other cities and towns throughout the South. In 1964, after another decade of protest, the US Congress finally passed the Civil Rights Act, which prohibited discrimination in employment, public services, and commerce and brought an end to legal segregation in Montgomery once and for all. This culminating victory was possible because of the lessons learned in Montgomery through thirteen months of experimentation, sacrifice, and personal and collective transformation.

NOTES

This chapter draws extensively from interviews of Rev. Lawson and guest speakers that were held during a special topics course sponsored by the Labor Center, the César E. Chávez Department of Chicana/o Studies, the Labor and Workplace Studies Minor, the Department of African American Studies, and the History Department at UCLA. Martin Luther King Jr.'s speeches, letters, and other documents are available online through the King Papers Project at Stanford University; http://mlk-kpp01.stanford.edu/primarydocuments/Vol4/3-Nov-1958_FromLawson.pdf.

1. James M. Lawson Jr., "The Philosophy of Nonviolence" (lecture, University of California, Los Angeles, April 17, 2013).

2. King used the phrase "the tools of justice" in his speech at Holt Street Baptist Church on December 5, 1955. See Martin Luther King Jr., "MIA Mass Meeting at Holt Street Baptist Church," King Papers, Martin Luther King Jr. Research and Education Institute, Stanford University, http://mlk-kpp01.stanford.edu/kingweb/publications/papers/vol3/551205.004-MIA_Mass_Meeting_at_Holt_Street_Baptist_Church.htm.

3. Donnie Williams, with Wayne Greenhaw, *The Thunder of Angels: The Montgomery Bus Boycott and the People Who Broke the Back of Jim Crow* (Chicago: Lawrence Hill Books, 2006), 41.

4. Jo Ann Robinson, *The Montgomery Bus Boycott and the Women Who Started It: The Memoir of Jo Ann Gibson Robinson*, ed. David J. Garrow (Knoxville: University of Tennessee Press, 1987), 8.

5. Quoted in Danielle L. McGuire, "At the Dark End of the Street: Sexualized Violence, Community Mobilization and the African American Freedom Struggle" (PhD diss., Rutgers University, 2007), 115.

6. Manning Marable, *The Third Reconstruction: Black Nationalism and Race Relations after the Revolution* (Dayton: Black Research Associates, 1980), 9; and Michael Perman, *Struggle for Mastery: Disenfranchisement in the South, 1888–1908* (Chapel Hill: University of North Carolina Press, 2001).

7. Leon F. Litwack, "Hellhounds," in *Without Sanctuary: Lynching Photography in America*, ed. James Allen (Santa Fe: Twin Palms Publishers, 2000), 12; and Stewart E. Tolnay and E. M. Beck, *Festival of Violence: An Analysis of Southern Lynching, 1882–1930* (Champaign: University of Illinois Press, 1995), 37.

8. For "tools of psychological and physical intimidation," see McGuire, "At The Dark End of the Street," 3; for "cheapness of black life," see Litwack, "Hellhounds," 12.

9. James M. Lawson Jr., "The Philosophy of Nonviolence" (lecture, University of California, Los Angeles, January 9, 2013).

10. Douglas Brinkley, *Rosa Parks* (New York: Viking, 2000), 34. A description of "Bogge Homa" appears in Williams and Greenhaw, *Thunder of Angels*, 5.

11. See Russell Barta, "The Domestic Worker: An Occupational Type" (master's thesis, Loyola University Chicago, 1947), 38–40, Loyala eCommons, http://ecommons.luc.edu/luc_theses/44. Barta analyzed wage rates as advertised in local newspapers in Birmingham in 1946 and showed that while some wages were as high at sixty dollars per week, most African American domestics in Birmingham made around thirteen to sixteen dollars per week, and some as little as two dollars a day.

12. Phillip Hoose, *Claudette Colvin: Twice toward Justice* (New York: Farrar, Straus & Giroux, 2009), 48.

13. Robinson, *Montgomery Bus Boycott*, 16.

14. Ibid., 35.

15. Ibid., 22.

16. McGuire emphasizes the power of black women's testimonials in "At the Dark End of the Street."

17. Hoose, *Claudette Colvin*, 23.

18. Martin Luther King Jr., *Stride toward Freedom: The Montgomery Story* (New York: Harper & Brothers, 1958), 34.

19. Jennifer L. Ritterhouse, *Growing Up Jim Crow: How Black and White Southern Children Learned Race* (Chapel Hill: University of North Carolina Press, 2006), 56–57; see also Blair L. M. Kelley, *Right to Ride: Streetcar Boycotts and African American Citizenship in the Era of Plessy v. Ferguson* (Chapel Hill: University of North Carolina Press, 2010).

20. Brinkley, *Rosa Parks*, 50–51.

21. King, *Stride toward Freedom*, 34–38.

22. Hoose, *Claudette Colvin*, 48–49. Parks is quoted in McGuire, "At the Dark End of the Street," 132–34.

23. Quoted in McGuire, "At the Dark End of the Street," 75. Nixon told Robinson, "You've got to think about the newspapers, you got to think about public opinion, you got to think policies and so forth, and intimidation" (ibid.).

24. Robinson, *Montgomery Bus Boycott*, 40.

25. Ibid., 42–44.

26. Quoted in McGuire, "At the Dark End of the Street," 143–44; and Robinson, *Montgomery Bus Boycott*, 45–46.

27. Quoted in Williams and Greenhaw, *Thunder of Angels*, 82.

28. Quoted in King, *Stride toward Freedom*, 60–61.

29. McGuire, "At the Dark End of the Street," 94.

30. King, "MIA Mass Meeting."

31. Lawson's explanation of agape is from "Nashville Sit-in Movement" (lecture, University of California, Los Angeles, January 23, 2013).

32. King, *Stride toward Freedom*, 85.

33. Robinson, *Montgomery Bus Boycott*, 91–93.

34. Quoted in ibid., 60.

35. Robinson refers to the "walking contingent" in *Montgomery Bus Boycott*, 114.

36. King, *Stride toward Freedom*, 87.

37. McGuire describes this in "At the Dark End of the Street," 94, 165.

38. Robinson, *Montgomery Bus Boycott*, 60; see also King, *Stride toward Freedom*, 86.

39. Brinkley, *Rosa Parks*, 151–52.

40. The case originally had five defendants, but Jeanetta Reese dropped her name from the suit after being pressured by local authorities.

41. Williams and Greenhaw, *Thunder of Angels*, 85.

42. Brinkley, *Rosa Parks*, 153–54.

43. King, *Stride toward Freedom*, 137–38.

44. Quoted in McGuire, "At the Dark End of the Street," 161–62.

45. See Kelley, *Right to Ride*.

46. Robinson's description of the arrests appears in *Montgomery Bus Boycott*, 150–54.

47. Ibid.

48. Martin Luther King Jr., "Testimony in State of Alabama v. M. L. King, Jr." (trial trascript, Montgomery, March 19–22, 1956), King Papers, Martin Luther King Jr. Research and Education Institute, Stanford University, https://kinginstitute.stanford.edu/king-papers/documents/testimony-state-alabama-v-m-l-king-jr.

49. Martin Luther King Jr., "Statement on Ending the Bus Boycott" (speech, Montgomery, December 20, 1956), King Papers, Martin Luther King Jr. Research and Education Institute, Stanford University, https://kinginstitute.stanford.edu/king-papers/documents/statement-ending-bus-boycott.

50. Quoted in Robinson, *Montgomery Bus Boycott*, 156–57.

51. Gandhi led the protestors from Ahmedabad to the coastal town of Dandi. Known alternately as the Salt Satyagrah, the Salt March, and the Dandi March, it lasted twenty-four days.

52. Brinkley, *Rosa Parks*, 159.

53. King, "Statement on Ending the Bus Boycott."

54. Quoted in Williams and Greenhaw, *Thunder of Angels*, 255.

55. Lawson, "Nashville Sit-in Movement."

56. Quoted in Williams and Greenhaw, *Thunder of Angels*, 48.

57. Lawson, "Philosophy of Nonviolence," January 9, 2013.

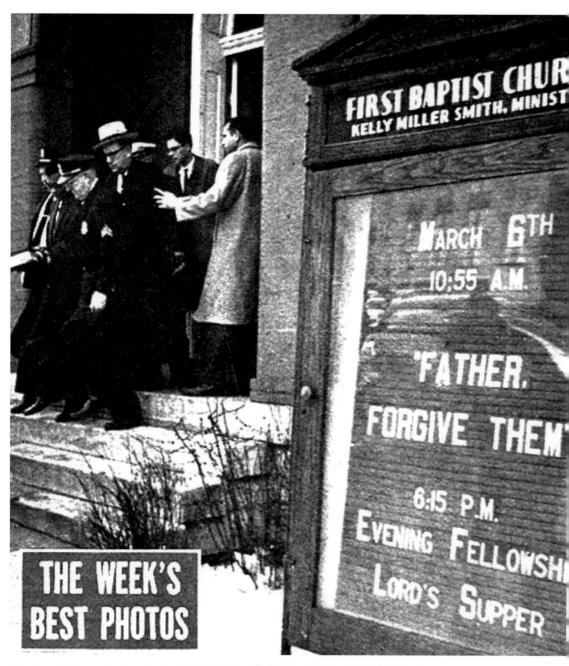

Rev. James M. Lawson Jr. is arrested on March 3, 1960, at the First Baptist Church in Nashville for his role in the sit-ins. *Photograph by Vic Cooley for the* Nashville Banner. *Courtesy of the Nashville Public Library, Special Collections.*

CHAPTER 3

THE NASHVILLE SIT-INS: A MODEL FOR A MOVEMENT

Caitlin Parker

The Nashville sit-in campaign brought national and international attention to the desegregation movement in the South. Although the news cameras captured the determination and resolve of students as they sat at "whites only" lunch counters in downtown Nashville, the media failed to capture the weeks of organizing and preparation that had made the protests possible. Far from a spontaneous student movement, the sit-ins were carefully shaped by Rev. James M. Lawson Jr.'s philosophy of nonviolence and supported by a broad community mobilization led by the Nashville Christian Leadership Council (NCLC). As Lawson explained, the success of the sit-ins depended on "fierce discipline and training. And strategizing and planning. And recruiting and doing the kinds of things you have to do to have a movement. That can't happen spontaneously. It has to happen systematically."[1]

When Lawson moved to Nashville, nonviolence had not yet become the guiding principle of direct-action campaigns, and many doubted that the success of the Montgomery bus boycott could be replicated. Lawson was determined to prove that nonviolence was not only effective but also essential to building the individual dignity and community solidarity that would be needed to sustain the movement for justice. Lawson's strategy of nonviolence became the model for nonviolent actions across the South. Veterans of the Nashville campaign subsequently lent their support to another campaign, the Freedom Rides, which resulted in a brutal test of their training and proved once again the power of nonviolence.

BUILDING A CAMPAIGN IN NASHVILLE

On February 6, 1957, Lawson shook hands with Dr. Martin Luther King Jr. at Oberlin College, and the two men had a conversation that changed the course of the struggle for racial justice in the United States. The timing of the meeting was fortuitous. Both King and Lawson were twenty-eight years old. Both were eager to overturn the immoral and unconstitutional Jim Crow laws and end the violence used to uphold them, and both were persuaded that nonviolence was the tool that could make that happen. Lawson had been working as a campus minister and coach at Hislop College in India and studying the teachings of Mohandas Gandhi when he read about the Montgomery bus boycott on the front page of the *Nagpur Times*. It was the first time he had heard of King, who had just finished leading the boycott. Lawson was eager to apply what he had learned to the civil rights struggle. He returned to the United States and enrolled in the Graduate School of Theology at Oberlin.

The boycott, which ended when the US Supreme Court ruled that segregation on public buses was unconstitutional, had demonstrated the strength of a people's movement and the power of nonviolent resistance. King hoped to replicate the success of the boycott and launch nonviolent direct action campaigns across the South. He recognized that the movement needed Lawson, who had a deep understanding of the philosophy of nonviolence. King encouraged Lawson to leave his graduate studies and to move south immediately. "[King] said, 'Come now. Don't wait. We don't have anyone like you in the South,'" Lawson recalled. "He meant the fact that I had had maybe ten, eleven years of study of nonviolence, experimenting with nonviolence. . . . He knew that he didn't have a black clergy person who had that kind of background."[2]

Lawson told A. J. Muste of the Fellowship of Reconciliation (FOR) of his plans, and in the fall of 1957 Muste hired him as FOR's southern field secretary. Lawson then spoke with Rev. Glenn Smiley, a white Methodist minister and field director for FOR, who had consulted with King during the Montgomery bus boycott. After speaking with Smiley, Lawson decided to go to Nashville, where he could resume his divinity studies at Vanderbilt University. The two agreed that Nashville had a more moderate racial climate than many of the other major Southern cities. For example, the local newspaper, the *Nashville Tennessean*, dedicated more coverage to black affairs than the newspapers in Atlanta, and white segregationist organizations were not as strong. Most important, however, was Nashville's municipal code. "Nashville had segregation, but there were no laws sustaining segregation," Lawson said. "It was enforced by intimidation and fear and police. . . . You did not have to go to court to overthrow laws in relationship to Jim Crow."[3]

While technically based in Nashville, Lawson's new position with FOR required him to travel across the southeast United States, counseling local groups in crisis situations, teaching nonviolence, and building momentum for a broader movement. In his role as a "troubleshooter," he visited the Little Rock Nine in Arkansas and traveled to Charlottesville, Columbia, Baton Rouge, and Birmingham.[4] Everywhere he went, Lawson distributed a comic book produced by the FOR that highlighted the African American community's use of nonviolent protest in the Montgomery bus boycott. As he met with various groups and local movement leaders, Lawson observed that many were excited by the events in Montgomery and eager to challenge the status quo, but they were not certain what the next step should be. Lawson realized that more work was needed to establish nonviolence as the most effective way of challenging Jim Crow.

> I began to become very much aware that the notion of nonviolent struggle and action was on the line. It happened in Montgomery, but can it happen in another way, in a different fashion? Is it a useful device, useful theory, useful methodology that has power to help people gain power and help turn their conditions and the conditions of the nation in a direction far more hopeful?[5]

To demonstrate the applicability of nonviolence as a theory and methodology, Lawson decided to make Nashville the site of the next direct action campaign. He wanted to prove that the Montgomery bus boycott was not a fluke, that its campaign of strategic nonviolence could be replicated.

Nashville turned out to be a wise choice for this test of nonviolence because an extraordinary group of African American religious leaders had converged there. Lawson described the coming together of so many committed, talented people as "providential," an example of God working through people to bring about a desired effect.[6] "I came to Nashville and found a community of faith which took me in as a fellow sojourner and gave me opportunities to use the tools I had been given and the skills I had learned," he noted.[7] In particular, Lawson reached out to Rev. Kelly Miller Smith and other leaders of the NCLC, including Rev. C. T. Vivian, Rev. Andrew White, Hellyn B. Johns, and Maeola Darden. Established in January 1958, the NCLC was a local affiliate of the Southern Christian Leadership Conference (SCLC).[8] Smith invited Lawson to be the director of the NCLC's Action Committee.

The NCLC found allies among progressive white theologians and religious organizations in Nashville. The Presbyterian Church had opened an office on racial progress, and whites opposed to segregation were involved in the Tennessee Council on Human Relations and the Nashville Community Relations Council. Lawson also found support from white colleagues such as Rev. Will D. Campbell and Dr. Everett Tilson. Campbell worked for the National Council of Churches and had participated in the founding of the SCLC. Tilson was a Methodist pastor teaching at Vanderbilt who had written a book refuting the idea that the Bible called for segregation. Both provided a base of support for Lawson's activism in Nashville.

Lawson's extensive knowledge of the philosophy of nonviolence decisively shaped the newly formed NCLC. Like Lawson, Smith hoped to employ Christian love in the fight against racism. The NCLC mission statement declared, "If we are to see the real downfall of segregation and discrimination it will be because of a disciplined Negro Christian movement which breaks the antiquated methods of resolving our fears and tensions and drastically applies the gospel we profess."[9] Yet it was not until Lawson and Smiley held a weeklong workshop with the NCLC in March 1958 that the group adopted nonviolence as its guiding principle.[10] Smith later said that before Lawson became involved, nonviolence was not discussed as a strategy or tactic.[11] "Jim [Lawson] was really the only person who was not a neophyte in this matter of nonviolence," Smith recalled. "He lived it and breathed it; it was his true philosophy."[12]

By the fall of 1958 Lawson had enrolled in Vanderbilt Divinity School and was ready to begin the process of planning a direct action campaign in Nashville. Lawson proposed that the NCLC begin with the question "What can we do in the city of Nashville from the perspective of Christian nonviolence structured by Gandhian understandings?"[13] Churches were the only places where the African American community could meet to plan its challenge to Jim Crow. They offered organizational resources, meeting spaces, and institutional support for the nascent movement. From January to June 1959, the NCLC discussed what direction the nonviolent struggle should take, in Nashville and nationally, in weekly Saturday meetings at local African American churches.[14] Lawson stated that "[we were] looking at ourselves, looking at our plight, looking at what are the possibilities for changing these conditions." The weekly church meetings "gave me a stunning picture of life that you could not get from the *Nashville Tennessean* or at the Vanderbilt University Divinity School," Lawson said.[15]

Previous desegregation campaigns had largely focused on schools, but the participants in the church meetings brought up issues of racism that they experienced in daily life. Lawson and the congregants quickly developed a comprehensive list of problems facing African Americans in Nashville. Lawson was especially affected by the testimony of black women who attended the workshops to express their concerns. "I had no idea how those workshops would come out. But it was the Negro women who prevailed upon what needed to be done," he said. "They talked about the indignity of having to shop in downtown Nashville and always risking insult and hostility coming from unexpected quarters." The women listed the racist policies of Woolworth, Harvey's, Cain-Sloan, and McLellans department stores, which would not allow black customers to try on clothes or shoes before purchasing them. Stores had segregated restrooms and drinking fountains—designated either "White" or "Colored"—if they had facilities for African Americans at all. The lunch counters were "whites only," meaning that women had no place to sit down and catch their breath or feed their children. "[The women] said to us boldly, 'You have no idea because you do not shop downtown. You have no idea the indignity we face when we have to do shopping for the family.' That was how the decision was made to begin downtown," Lawson explained.[16]

Until the Montgomery bus boycott, the evolving civil rights movement had focused primarily on schools and legal action to make segregation unconstitutional. People in Nashville now decided to attack the hostility of public segregation through a grassroots action. This was a major strategic change that promoted the development of the nonviolent movement. Once the NCLC had reached a consensus on targeting downtown Nashville, Lawson created a plan for a series of workshops on nonviolence, which began in September 1959.

> The purpose of the workshop from day one was to desegregate downtown Nashville. To use the sit-in, to use picketing, to use economic boycott and other tactics as necessary, but to begin with the sit-in. I then prepared the workshops based upon that determination to start a movement, a campaign, that was to show that the Montgomery bus boycott and Martin King's adoption of the language of nonviolence . . . could be done again.[17]

TEACHING AND TRAINING IN NONVIOLENCE

Recognizing that students had more time to dedicate to the desegregation campaign than working adults, Lawson recruited students from the nearby colleges. The workshops were held on Tuesday nights in the basement of Clark Memorial Methodist Church, close to Fisk University. Paul LaPrad, a white transfer student at Fisk who was eager to get involved in nonviolent protest, helped Lawson spread the word on the Fisk campus. One of LaPrad's first recruits was Diane Nash, an African American student from Chicago who was appalled by the more overt racial segregation of the South. Lawson also enlisted students like Pauline Knight, Curtis Murphy, and Lester McKinney from Tennessee Agricultural and Industrial University (renamed Tennessee State University in 1968). Eighteen-year-old John Lewis heard about the workshops from Smith, his professor at American Baptist College, and he recruited his classmates Bernard Lafayette, James Bevel, and others. The workshops held immediate appeal for a younger generation frustrated by the segregation and the hostility that they met in Nashville. "We had been talking about these problems of segregation even before the workshops had started. That's why it was easy to recruit me," Lafayette recalled. "Now we're talking about doing something about it. And that was what was so exciting, to be able take action."[18]

Lawson's first task was to convince the students that nonviolence was a viable and essential strategy. At that time Lawson was the most highly trained nonviolence organizer in the United States, and he was eager to see the tactics of nonviolence spread throughout the freedom struggle. Yet many students were skeptical. "I thought nonviolence would not work," Nash later said. "But I stayed for one reason and that was because it was the only game in town."[19] Lawson used the initial workshops to explain the power of nonviolence. Though the students might feel powerless individually, and their numbers might start out small, the moral righteousness of their cause would force people on the sidelines to act. He assured the students that their sacrifice in pursuit of equality would inspire others to join the movement. Nonviolence worked because it was "a demonstration of power," Lawson asserted. "Not economic power. Not military power. But social power. The power of people united around a common purpose."[20] To be nonviolent was to be militant in creating change.

Lawson rooted nonviolence in biblical scripture, the life of Jesus, and the concept of love. This biblical foundation appealed to the students, many of whom had grown up

One of the things I lifted up, and I still do in teachings and trainings . . . is that **religion at its best tries to get human beings**. . . to accept their fundamental humanity and **take responsibility for the management and control of their anger**, for their fear, for their animosities. To not pretend it comes from somebody else. **To develop a spiritual life**, whereby you can be in a very hostile situation, but you can still try to shape your own life because it is a gift, and there is no gift exactly like that. And you can mold it.

—Rev. Lawson April 2013

attending church with their families.[21] The biblical focus also reflected Lawson's own path to nonviolence. In particular, Lawson drew from chapter 5 of the book of Matthew. Jesus's rejection of the status quo and his decision to love his enemies had greatly impressed Lawson as a young student.

> I found it as a strategic kit. Jesus is saying, though these are not his words but my paraphrase, if you live in the Roman Empire, which is a pretty terrible occupation of our land, you do not have to become a Roman Empire supporter. You do not have to act that way. You have a kind of singular autonomy that you can decide you're going to resist the wrongdoer, the evildoer. You're not going to retaliate.[22]

Lawson dedicated a significant portion of the workshops to helping the participants realize that they had the autonomy to break unjust laws and practice a healing love. One of the first assignments was to talk about love and how it could be used as a tactic. Lawson told participants that they had to recognize their own internal strength and dignity before they could face oppressors. In order to practice nonviolence, Lawson explained, the students needed to "accept their fundamental humanity and take responsibility for the management and control of their anger, of their fear, of their animosities, to not pretend it comes from someone else." Only after that acceptance could they "develop an inward mental life, intellectual life, and spiritual life, whereby you can be in a very hostile situation, but you can still try to shape your own life because it is a gift and there is no gift exactly like that."[23] Lafayette explained that "this nonviolence was not just a workshop that Jim Lawson gave, it was transformation starting with the individuals."[24]

By recognizing their own power to channel anger and frustration into creative nonviolent action, the workshop participants could begin to build a "beloved community," the realization of God's kingdom on earth. A Christian concept emphasized by both Lawson and King, the beloved community connoted both an ideal state to strive for and a sense of solidarity in the struggle. Lawson also introduced participants to Gandhi's methodology and techniques of producing social, economic, and political change. Lawson began to read Gandhi in 1947, the same year that he joined FOR. From Gandhi,

That passion for **readdressing the wrong was a very important part** of the ethos of our time that made it work.
—Rev. Lawson April 2013

Lawson learned that nonviolence was love in action and "always connected to strategies and blueprints for change."[25] Lawson taught participants about Gandhi's concept of nonviolent struggle and satyagraha, or "steadfastness in truth," the soul force that would carry protestors through suffering. Lewis noted that Lawson was "arming us, preparing us, planting in us a sense of both rightness and righteousness—'soul force'—that would see us through the ugliness and pain."[26]

Lawson taught participants about the march Gandhi led in 1930 to protest the British salt tax, a hated symbol of colonialism. Thousands of Indians walked 240 miles, demanding national self-determination and demonstrating that nonviolence is not passive or noncoercive. It is a form of militancy every bit as intense as armed warfare. "Gandhi showed that it could be done," Lewis recalled.

> This one little man armed with nothing but the truth and a fundamental faith in the response of human society to redemptive suffering, was able to reshape an entire nation without raising so much as a fist. And he did it not by aiming high, at the people in power, but by aiming low, at the downtrodden, the poor, the men and women and children who inhabited the streets and fields of his country.[27]

Lawson also stressed that although Gandhi had used the term *nonviolence*, the practice of nonviolence was not new. Lawson taught the participants about the antislavery movement and the economic boycotts and other acts of nonviolent protest during the American Revolution. He described sit-ins in Chicago, Los Angeles, and other cities in the early 1940s.[28] He also told stories about Norwegian and Danish opposition to the Nazi occupation during World War II. Learning about the history of nonviolence had a deep impact on the students. Lewis said that this historical perspective was invaluable.

> It was mind-blowing to learn that the tension between what was right and wrong that had torn at me since I was old enough to think had a historical context, that people of all cultures and all ages had struggled with the same questions, the same brutal realities that we were facing in 1950s America in terms of race, and that their responses, across thousands of miles and thousands of years, had much in common and much to show us about how to deal with the wrong we faced—the wrong of racial hatred and segregation. These were incredibly powerful ideas, and their beauty was that they applied to real life, to the specifics of the world we walked in.[29]

As the workshops progressed, Lawson increasingly focused on putting the principles of nonviolence into practice. He used role-playing to simulate the types of hostile and violent situations that protestors would face. For example, to teach participants how to confront physical violence, Lawson put them in pairs and had one person slap the other. The participants would then discuss how it felt to be either the perpetrator or the recipient of violence. Lawson also had participants stage mock sit-ins, in which they would sit on stools while others would take turns shouting insults, yelling racial epithets, blowing smoke in their faces, and slapping or pushing them. Lafayette recalled that the purpose of the training was to "give emotional conditioning, because it's one thing to tell someone intellectually, you know, you're gonna go down and you're not going to hit back." He noted that to participate in an exercise "where someone would slap and push you" took much more discipline. "And the thing that was so amazing to me is our role-play was exactly what happened when we got down there."[30]

In November, as the workshop participants gained experience, they began to hold test sit-ins at selected department stores, where the purpose was not to court arrest but to gain information from the store management about their policies. The test sit-ins allowed the participants to gauge the attitudes of downtown storeowners. The first test sit-in was on November 28 at Harveys. A small racially mixed group of students and clergy, all formally dressed, gathered at First Baptist Church to prepare. Members of the congregation drove the students to the department store, where they entered the lunchroom and sat at the counter. The students sat in a "color spectrum" in order of their skin tone. When the waitress realized it was a multiracial group and told them that they could not be served, Nash asked to speak to the manager. The manager explained that he was not in favor of segregation because refusing customers hurt the store's business, but that Harveys did not want to be the only store to desegregate. The group thanked him and left. On December 5 Lawson and a group of workshop participants staged a second test sit-in at Cain-Sloan, where they were refused service by the manager, who recited the store's policy of segregation. The owner, John Sloan, was an ardent segregationist, and he flatly refused to talk to the students.[31]

By the end of 1959 the students who would become leaders of the sit-ins—including Nash, Lafayette, Bevel, Lewis, LaPrad, McKinney, Murphy, Angeline Butler, Gloria Johnson, Jim Zwerg, Rodney Powell, Julius Scruggs, Paul Brooks, Catherine Burks, and Marion Barry—had bonded, forming the "beloved community" about which Lawson spoke. Though still fearful, students felt as prepared as they could be to face violence and arrest. Lafayette called their training under Lawson "a nonviolent academy equivalent to West Point."[32] The students also took on new responsibilities as the workshops swelled with new recruits. Soon Lawson began holding meetings on Thursday nights in a larger room at Clark Memorial Church in addition to the Tuesday night sessions.

LAUNCHING THE SIT-INS

Events outside Nashville pushed Lawson's group from the planning stage to execution. On February 1, 1960, four college freshmen in Greensboro held a sit-in at the lunch counter of the local Woolworth store. Local media were quick to dismiss the Greensboro sit-in as college prank "of the 'panty-raid variety.'"[33] While the sit-in seemed to be spontaneous, at least one of the students had read the FOR comic book on nonviolence.[34] The Greensboro sit-in inspired other student sit-ins, creating a trend that the media could not easily dismiss. Two days later Douglass Moore, a Methodist minister in Durham who knew of Lawson's workshops on nonviolence, asked Lawson to hold a sit-in in sympathy with the Greensboro Four. That Thursday seventy-five students and community members met to begin mobilizing for large-scale protests. Unlike the Greensboro students, the students in Nashville had extensive training and a base of community support. The action in Greenville jumpstarted the sit-in movement, but it was the Nashville campaign that established the strategy and fueled the sit-in movement nationally.

On February 13, 1960, 124 college students conducted sit-ins at the lunch counters of three stores in downtown Nashville. The students dressed in their Sunday best and brought books to occupy themselves. When the Woolworth staff closed the lunch counter and turned off the lights, the students stayed in their seats and did their homework until closing time. Kress and McLellans closed their lunch counters as well, and the white staff and customers appeared shaken by the students' presence. Nash described watching a nervous waitress drop dish after dish on the floor as the students sat at the counter. According to Lewis, who was among the students at Woolworth, the sit-in "couldn't have gone any more smoothly. When we got back to First Baptist, it was like New Year's Eve—whooping, cheering, hugging, laughing, singing. It was sheer euphoria, like a jubilee."[35] The extensive preparation and training had served the students well, but Lawson knew that to gain momentum and force a response from the white community, the sit-ins needed to attract larger and larger numbers. To Lawson's delight, once the sit-in leadership had demonstrated their preparation and purpose, students flocked to the movement.

As organizing progressed in February, Lawson proposed and formed a new group, the Central Committee, to develop a strategy for the campaign and promote leadership development. The NCLC was the parent body of the Central Committee, providing funding, transportation, and other guidance and logistical support. Nash served as the chair of the Central Committee, which included two student representatives from the campuses of Vanderbilt, Fisk, Tennessee Agricultural and Industrial University, and American Baptist College. The Central Committee always appointed both a student and an adult from the community, usually from the NCLC, to make public statements.

On February 18, several hundred students staged a second sit-in. Two days later 340 showed up to participate. After the initial sit-ins, the workshops began to grow so quickly that Lawson could not train everyone. "That I had not anticipated," Lawson said. "The people who followed us who hadn't been in the workshops saw character and saw courage and they saw people who had some inkling of what they were doing and were prepared to go to the ground."[36] Students held informal workshops with classmates interested in getting involved. To bring the newcomers up to speed, the Central Committee printed a primer on Lawson's teachings and how protestors should conduct themselves.

DO NOT:
1. Strike back nor curse if abused.
2. Lash out.
3. Hold conversations with floor walker.
4. Leave your seat until your leader has given you permission to do so.
5. Block entrances to stores outside nor the aisles inside.

DO:
1. Show yourself friendly and courteous at all times.
2. Sit straight; always face the counter.
3. Report all serious incidents to your leader.
4. Refer information seekers to your leader in a polite manner.
5. Remember the teachings of Jesus Christ, Mahatma Gandhi, and Martin Luther King. Love and nonviolence is the way.
MAY GOD BLESS EACH OF YOU[37]

Student leadership rotated, and each sit-in group chose a spokesperson as well as an observer to gauge the reactions of employees, bystanders, and the police. By the middle of February, the Central Committee was coordinating regular sit-ins, sometimes holding two a week.

Student leadership proved essential on February 27, when for the first time the sit-ins provoked a violent backlash and resulted in mass arrests. The students had learned in advance that the department stores had asked the city to stop the sit-ins. The NCLC requested a meeting with Nashville's mayor, Ben West, but he refused to see either the NCLC representatives or an independent biracial group of ministers who supported the sit-ins. The chief of police informed Lawson and members of the Central Committee that any future demonstrations would result in arrests. On the mayor's orders, the police department had begun to develop a legal justification for the arrests that included trespass and disturbing the peace. At previous sit-ins the officers had kept bystanders moving and prevented mobs from forming, but on February 27 they intentionally hung back.[38]

For the first time the students' principles of nonviolence were tested in the face of real violence. A large mob of vocal and violent counterprotesters formed at each of the sit-in locations. As a white sympathizer, LaPrad was one of the first students assaulted. A group of young white men dragged him from his stool and punched and kicked him as he lay on the floor of the restaurant.[39] White mobs threw food at the protestors, poured drinks down their shirts, put out cigarettes in their hair, yelled obscenities and racial slurs, and beat them. Police did not restrain or arrest the attackers. Instead, the officers approached the students and told them that if they did not vacate the stools, they would be arrested. None of the protestors fought back, and eighty were arrested and incarcerated.

The Central Committee had prepared for the arrests by planning to have multiple waves of protestors enter each store. Lawson had adapted this strategy from Gandhi's

Walgreens closes its lunch counter in February 1960, during the Nashville sit-ins. *Photograph by Vic Cooley for the* Nashville Banner. *Courtesy of the Nashville Public Library, Special Collections.*

Agitators attack protestors during a sit-in at a department store lunch counter in downtown Nashville, February 27, 1960. *Photograph by Vic Cooley for the* Nashville Banner. *Courtesy of the Nashville Public Library, Special Collections.*

nonviolent protest at the salt works at Dharasana, in which participants had marched in rows toward the police guarding the factory. Once one group had been beaten back by the police, another wave of marchers came up behind them. The purpose was to overwhelm the police, and the tactic had a similar impact at the Nashville lunch counters. Each time the police arrested a group of protestors for sitting at the whites-only counter, another set of protestors entered the restaurant to take their places.[40] Four hundred people participated in sit-ins at six lunch counters that day. Nash recalled that the number of students and their persistence "really surprised the police. They thought they had lowered the boom, and then they turned around and saw the lunch counter once again full of Negro students . . . and there was still another group waiting to take their place."[41] The police continued to arrest protestors, who quickly became a burden on the system. The protestors refused bail, overloading the jails, forcing officers to work overtime, and undermining the potency of incarceration to maintain segregation.

The campaign and mass arrests mobilized the African American community. Z. Alexander Looby, a well-known black lawyer in Nashville, organized his colleagues to defend the arrested protestors. The protestors declined to pay the fifty-dollar fine imposed by the judge and opted instead to serve thirty days of labor. On Sundays the ministers of the African American churches spoke out in support of the sit-ins and raised money to continue them. The churches also helped launch an economic boycott of segregated downtown stores that continued through the spring. Picketers held signs outside the stores declaring "Down with Jim Crowism," "Equal Rights for All," and "Dignity before Dollars." A Fisk economist estimated that 98 percent of Nashville's African American population participated in the boycott, and many whites also avoided the downtown shopping area, either out of solidarity or out of fear. Segregation cost the department stores an estimated 40 percent of their sales.[42]

The rapid community mobilization confirmed Lawson's belief that a latent desire for change existed in Nashville and across the South. One middle-aged African American woman reported, "Once we saw the students being herded into the patrol cars, I was just so moved that I went to the telephone immediately and began calling fifty people, asking them to call ten more, encouraging people not to trade downtown."[43] Nonviolent protest proved powerful because it allowed all members of the black community to contribute in their own fashion, whether by participating in the sit-ins or providing funding, facilities, transportation, or legal assistance.[44]

The arrests also sharpened the conflict between the protestors and the elites who wanted to maintain racial segregation. On February 29 Mayor West attended a meeting with members of the clergy at Smith's First Baptist Church. Lawson summarized the goals of the sit-in movement for the mayor, who insisted that the demonstrators had trespassed on private property. In response, Lawson argued that "in this instance, the law was a gimmick to intimidate, harass, and if possible, halt a legitimate movement of social concern and justice." As nonviolent demonstrators, he explained, the students accepted the consequences of breaking the law but stood by their refusal to follow an unjust law. West then accused Lawson of "calling for a blood bath in the streets of Nashville." Lawson recalled that the conservative newspaper *The Nashville Banner* ran a lead editorial that portrayed him as an "outside agitator" who was inciting anarchy by urging the students to break the law. That week Lawson was expelled from Vanderbilt, and on March 3 he was arrested on the charge of conspiring to disrupt business.[45]

On April 19 the Nashville Central Committee was preparing to meet when they learned that Looby's home had been bombed as a reprisal for defending the arrested students. The group immediately began to organize a four-mile silent march from the campus of Tennessee A & I to city hall. By the time the protestors reached city hall, the march had grown to include four thousand Nashville residents. "We held our heads high because we were right, and we knew we were walking for something right," Nash recalled. "We were really striding towards freedom."[46] The Central Committee had designated Nash and Vivian as the spokespeople for the march. Once the marchers reached city hall, Vivian approached West, who merely reiterated that he could not get involved because he could not violate the property rights of the storeowners.

Although Vivian and West had reached an impasse, Nash saw an opportunity to make a personal moral appeal to West. "Mayor West," she asked, "do you feel it is wrong to discriminate against a person solely on the basis of his race or color?" West conceded that he did. Nash then asked if he felt that the lunch counters should be desegregated, and West said yes. The workshops on nonviolence had encouraged Nash to understand her opponent. She knew that the mayor was in a tricky place politically, and she appealed to him publicly as a person who had expressed moderate views on Jim Crow and segregation practices. Lawson noted that Nash handled the moment perfectly.

> Diane, with the kind of character and intelligence that she had, was able to ask Mayor West a couple additional questions, in which for the first time the mayor said that it was wrong for us not to be served in these restaurants, which was the first time that any major official in the city had said that.[47]

Lawson and the Central Committee insisted on negotiating with the store managers and owners directly.[48] Aware that the owners would claim that they had no way to desegregate the stores, the committee members decided to show the store owners how it

The home of Nashville attorney and councilman Z. Alexander Looby after being bombed on the morning of April 19, 1960. *Photograph by Bob Ray for the* Nashville Banner. *Courtesy of the Nashville Public Library, Special Collections.*

Rev. Andrew White, Rev. C. T. Vivian, Diana Nash, Curtis Murphy, and other sit-in leaders confront Nashville's mayor, Ben West, on April 19, 1960. *Photograph by Vic Cooley for the* Nashville Banner. *Courtesy of the Nashville Public Library, Special Collections.*

ould be accomplished. The Central Committee assured the owners of six stores that there would be no public declaration of desegregation, and the storeowners agreed to remove the white and "colored" signs and to serve all customers on May 10. The Central Committee organized teams of two, mostly married couples, that would quietly test the desegregation of each store. When it was clear that integration had been achieved, the mass demonstrations would end. Lawson explained that the conclusion of nonviolent protest is as important as its inception.

> One of the important principles of nonviolence is that when you're able to develop a movement that can have a major change, a step towards justice, steps eradicating the harm—that that's a victory for everybody. It's no time to crow over victory and defeat. On the contrary, a part of the follow-up of the nonviolent movement is the business of reconciliation, that former opponents can become friends. That the opportunity for the enmity that may have been there to be dissipated, to be forgiven and for people to move on with a new life, a new relationship has to be permitted.[49]

The Central Committee's plan for desegregation proceeded without incident, and three weeks after the march to city hall, Nashville became the first major city in the South to begin the desegregation of public places.

The Nashville sit-ins provided the nonviolent organizing victory that King had hoped for when he urged Lawson to take his expertise to the South. At a speech at Fisk University, King called the Nashville movement "the best organized and most disciplined in the Southland." "I did not come to Nashville to bring inspiration," he declared, "but to gain inspiration from the great movement that has taken place in this community."[50] The Nashville movement became a model for the SCLC, the Student Nonviolent Coordinating Committee (SNCC), the National Association for the Advancement of Colored People (NAACP), and other groups that hoped to desegregate public life in cities such as Dallas and Memphis. The Nashville campaign not only proved that desegregation could occur but also provided a blueprint of key tactics for implementing a strategy of nonviolence. White business owners also learned by word of mouth that desegregation could be good for business. By the middle of the summer, twenty-seven cities had followed Nashville's example.[51]

Jim Crow did not disappear in these cities overnight. In Nashville organizers moved on to protest segregation in movie theaters, grocery stores, and other businesses. These struggles helped advance support for the 1964 Civil Rights Act, which prohibited discrimination or segregation in places of public accommodation. Segregation continued despite the law, as whites actively tried to bar African Americans from public places and maintained the exclusivity of private spaces. Taking inspiration from the Montgomery bus boycott and the Nashville sit-ins, new organizations continued the struggle to gain equal recognition under the law and fair treatment in practice.

FROM THE SIT-INS TO THE FREEDOM RIDES

Lawson's teachings inspired the rise of a national student movement. In early April 1960, the SCLC convened a meeting at Shaw University in Raleigh, which led to the formation of the SNCC. Lawson delivered the keynote address at the meeting. His teachings provided the foundation for the SNCC, and the SNCC's mission statement affirmed the group's commitment to nonviolence and emphasized the transformative power of love.[52] The education and experience that the Nashville students had gained from Lawson's workshops set them apart from their peers. Other students recalled being impressed with the self-assurance,

A protester boycotts downtown businesses in Nashville in the spring of 1960. *Photograph by Vic Cooley for the* Nashville Banner. *Courtesy of the Nashville Public Library, Special Collections.*

leadership, and independence of the Nashville group. Julian Bond, one of the students who helped establish the SNCC, recalled,

> I was very taken by their group personality, not just their panache and the confidence they had in each other, but how far they had already gone. Unlike [the students from Atlanta], they had really taken over the leadership of the sit-ins in Nashville. The older ministers there had been very good in giving them their head and they were making all the critical decisions themselves.[53]

Nash served as the first field representative of the SNCC, and Barry was appointed president; he was followed by Lewis.[54]

After the conclusion of the sit-in campaign, the Nashville students lent their support to the Freedom Rides, ensuring that the momentum of the Nashville protests would continue.[55] The first Freedom Ride was launched by the Congress of Racial Equality (CORE) in the spring of 1961. Two buses were to travel through the South, from Washington, DC, to New Orleans, to test whether interstate bus lines and bus stations were complying with federal desegregation orders. The integrated group of Freedom Riders crossed Georgia without a serious incident, but once the riders reached Alabama, on May 14, white opposition turned violent. When the first bus pulled into the station at Anniston, it was met by a mob composed mainly of members of the White Citizens' Council and the Ku Klux Klan, who had been alerted by the local police. Members of the mob carrying baseball bats, pipes, and other makeshift weapons broke windows and slashed tires, but they were unable to enter the bus. Anniston police finally stepped in and escorted the damaged bus to the city limits, followed by a long line of cars and trucks filled with members of the mob. A few miles outside of town, flat tires forced the bus driver to pull over, and the mob attacked again. The bus was firebombed, forcing the passengers to flee the burning bus before it exploded.

The second bus reached Birmingham, where it was met by a mob of Klansmen and members of the extremist National States Rights Party who brutally beat the Freedom Riders as they entered the bus terminal. State and federal authorities knew in advance that the Freedom Riders would be attacked, but they did nothing to intervene. The US attorney general, Robert Kennedy, called for a "cooling off period" and blamed "extremists on both sides" for the violence. The governor of Alabama, John Patterson, refused to provide police protection for the continuation of the bus journey to Montgomery, and plans to fly the Freedom Riders to New Orleans were initially thwarted by a bomb threat. Finally, on May 15, late at night, the freedom riders boarded a plane for New Orleans. The Freedom Rides appeared to be derailed.[56]

Leaders from the Nashville group sensed the danger in allowing mob violence to defeat nonviolence at this crucial juncture. After a fierce debate, Lewis, Nash, Lafayette, and others from the Central Committee decided to step forward and resume the Freedom Rides. "We can't let them stop us with violence," Nash declared. "If we do, the movement is dead."[57] Lawson remembered this as the first moment that the Central Committee recognized that nonviolent resistance had become a national effort. "Chances are if we hadn't done that," Lawson speculated, "it would have been quite some time before any major activity took place to ignite the movement again."[58]

On May 17, after writing wills and letters to loved ones, the group of Central Committee volunteers left Nashville on a bus that was bound for Montgomery. The riders were arrested in Birmingham for defying segregation laws, driven to the Tennessee border, and dumped at the side of the road. They made their way back, reaching Birmingham on May 19, where they waited another day until pressure from the Kennedy administration forced the provision of a bus and police protection. The riders boarded the bus on Mother's

Painting by Charlotta Janssen of the booking photograph
taken when Rev. James M. Lawson Jr. was arrested in
Jackson for his participation in the Freedom Rides. *Courtesy
of Charlotta Janssen.*

Day, May 20, and the Freedom Ride resumed. As the bus neared Montgomery, the police escort vanished, and when the riders disembarked at the station, a large white mob that included women and children attacked the riders with broken bottles, lead pipes, and baseball bats. Police did not attempt to bring the bloody riot under control until several hours later, at which point over twenty people had been seriously injured, including reporters and federal official John Seigenthaler.

Urged by Nash, SNCC and SCLC leaders, including King, traveled to Montgomery to hold a rally at Rev. Ralph Abernathy's First Baptist Church on May 21. The white crowd that gathered outside the church proved so violent that federal marshals equipped with tear gas could barely contain them. Robert Kennedy pleaded with movement leaders to give up the Freedom Rides, but they refused. The governor of Mississippi, Ross Barnett, vowed to uphold "law and order" against the "outside agitators."[59]

Lawson drove to Montgomery with five volunteers to join the Freedom Riders, almost half of whom were Nashville veterans, for the next portion of the trip, which would take them to Jackson. Lawson held a nonviolence workshop on the bus.[60] When the Freedom Riders arrived in Jackson, they were arrested by Mississippi officials. The riders refused bail, and Nashville veteran Knight announced that there would be "another busload from Nashville" ready to take up the route. Mississippi officials attempted to break the will of the riders by transporting them from the city's jails to the notorious Parchman Farm (Mississippi State Penitentiary), a rural institution away from federal oversight, where state officials could violently discipline the protestors. The Freedom Riders turned Parchman into a school of nonviolence, holding workshops, sharing stories of successful local campaigns, and singing freedom songs. Despite the jailers' best efforts to bankrupt the riders of money and morale, the Freedom Riders' time in prison planted the seeds for new movements. The NCLC, along with the SCLC, CORE, SNCC, and the National Student Association, formed the Freedom Ride Coordinating Committee and established centers in Nashville, Atlanta, New Orleans, Jackson, and Los Angeles, recruiting new participants in an all-out assault on Jim Crow.

The strategy of nonviolence that was pioneered in the Montgomery bus boycott, proven in the Nashville sit-ins, and applied in the Freedom Rides provoked massive resistance and brought the racial status quo in the South to the breaking point. Nonviolent direct action worked because protestors rejected the terms of an unjust peace and proved that they were willing to suffer and die for the cause of racial equality. In the summer of 1961, Lawson declared,

> Only when this hostility comes to the surface . . . as it did in Montgomery and Birmingham, will we begin to see that the system of segregation is an evil which destroys people and teaches them a contempt for life. We are trying to reach the conscience of the South. Brutality must be suffered to show the true character of segregation.[61]

In subsequent years, participants in Lawson's Nashville workshops spread throughout the country, implementing his teachings on nonviolence. The overarching principle of nonviolence sustained the movement through disagreements and organizational rivalries. Veterans of the Nashville sit-ins went on to lead the Albany movement in 1961, the Birmingham campaign and the March on Washington in 1963, Freedom Summer in 1964, the marches from Selma to Montgomery in 1965, and other crucial direct-action campaigns.

NOTES

This chapter draws extensively from interviews of Rev. Lawson and guest speakers that were held during a special topics course sponsored by the Labor Center, the César E. Chávez Department of Chicana/o Studies, the Labor and Workplace Studies Minor, the Department of African American Studies, and the History Department at UCLA.

1. Peter Ackerman and Jack Duvall, "The Nashville Sit-in Movement," *A Force More Powerful*, DVD, directed by Steve York (Washington, DC: York Zimmerman Inc., 2000).

2. James M. Lawson Jr., "Seeking First the Kingdom: The Nashville Story, 1958–1962," YouTube video, 1:38:33, Cole Lecture, Vanderbilt University, October 15, 2009, posted by Vanderbilt University, http://www.youtube.com/watch?v=whSYy1Iy-HI; see also James M. Lawson Jr., "Interview: Rev. James Lawson," Nashville 1960: *We Were Warriors*, part 1 of *A Force More Powerful: A Century of Nonviolent Conflict*, broadcast on PBS, September 18, 2000, http://web.archive.org/web/20041209111131 /http://www.pbs.org/weta/forcemorepowerful/nashville/interview.html.

3. James M. Lawson Jr., "A Conversation with James Lawson," YouTube video, 23:46, posted by WPNT, Nashville Public Television, November 9, 2009, http://www.youtube.com/watch?v=8SMLebhfPE8.

4. Barry Everett Lee, "The Nashville Civil Rights Movement: A Study of the Phenomenon of Intentional Leadership Development and Its Consequences for Local Movements and the National Civil Rights Movement" (PhD diss., Georgia State University, 2010), 8, http://scholarworks.gsu.edu/cgi/viewcontent.cgi ?article=1015&context=history_diss.

5. Lawson, "Seeking First the Kingdom."

6. David Halberstam, *The Children* (New York: Random House, 1998), 51.

7. Lawson, "Seeking First the Kingdom."

8. Nashville Christian Leadership Council, *Toward the Beloved Community: Story of the Nashville Christian Leadership Council* (Nashville: Nashville Christian Leadership Council, 1961), crmvet.org, http:// www.crmvet.org/docs/61_nclc.pdf.

9. See John Lewis, *Walking with the Wind: A Memoir of the Movement* (New York: Simon and Schuster, 1998), 74.

10. Nashville Christian Leadership Council, *Toward the Beloved Community*.

11. Smith is quoted by Lee, "Nashville Civil Rights Movement," 123.

12. Kelly Miller Smith, interview by Robert Penn Warren, February 13, 1964, transcript, Robert Penn Warren Civil Rights Oral History Project, University of Kentucky Special Collections, Lexington. See also "Kelly Miller Smith," *Robert Penn Warren's "Who Speaks for the Negro": An Archival Collection*, website, http://whospeaks.library.vanderbilt.edu/interview/kelly-miller-smith.

13. Lawson, "Seeking First the Kingdom."

14. Lawson, "A Conversation with James Lawson."

15. Lawson, "Seeking First the Kingdom"; and Lawson, "A Conversation with James Lawson."

16. Ibid.

17. James M. Lawson Jr. and Bernard Lafayette, discussion with Kent Wong and Kelly Lytle Hernandez, April 24, 2013, Los Angeles.

18. Lawson and Lafayette, discussion with Wong and Hernandez.

19. Quoted in Ackerman and Duvall, "The Nashville Sit-in Movement" (DVD).

20. Lawson and Lafayette, discussion with Wong and Hernandez.

21. Lawson, "Seeking First the Kingdom"; and Lawson, "A Conversation with James Lawson."

22. Lawson and Lafayette, discussion with Wong and Lytle Hernandez.

23. Ibid.

24. Ibid.

25. James M. Lawson Jr., "James Lawson—Gandhi and Nonviolence," YouTube video, 3:36, posted by International Center on Nonviolent Conflict, September 30, 2010, http://www.youtube.com/watch?v=Q8K4HLM03dw.

26. Lewis, *Walking with the Wind*, 86.

27. Ibid. The march is known by several names: Salt Satyagrah, the Salt March, and the Dandi March.

28. Lawson and Lafayette, discussion with Wong and Hernandez.

29. Lewis, *Walking with the Wind*, 79.

30. Lawson and Lafayette, discussion with Wong and Hernandez.

31. Lewis, *Walking with the Wind*, 96.

32. Quoted in Peter Ackerman and Jack Duvall, *A Force More Powerful: A Century of Nonviolent Conflict* (New York: Palgrave, 2000), 316.

33. Claude Sitton, "Negro Sitdowns Stir Fear of Wider Unrest in the South," *New York Times*, February 14, 1960, http://www.nytimes.com/learning/general/onthisday/big/0201.html.

34. Larry Isaac, "Movement of Movements: Culture Moves in the Long Civil Rights," *Social Forces* 87, no. 1 (2008): 33–63.

35. Lewis, *Walking with the Wind*, 103–4.

36. Lawson and Lafayette, discussion with Wong and Hernandez.

37. Lewis, *Walking with the Wind*, 106–7.

38. James Lawson, interview by Robert Penn Warren, March 17, 1964, transcript, Robert Penn Warren Civil Rights Oral History Project, University of Kentucky Special Collections, Lexington. See also "James M. Lawson Jr.," *Robert Penn Warren's "Who Speaks for the Negro": An Archival Collection*, website, http://whospeaks.library.vanderbilt.edu/interview/james-m-lawson-jr.

39. Ackerman and Duvall, "Nashville Sit-in Movement" (DVD).

40. James M. Lawson Jr., "Nashville Sit-in Movement" (lecture, University of California, Los Angeles, January 23, 2013).

41. Ackerman and Duvall, "Nashville Sit-in Movement" (DVD).

42. Ibid. See also NBC News, "NBC News Special: White Paper: Sit-In," NBC broadcast, December 20, 1960, http://www.nbcuniversalarchives.com/nbcuni/clip/51A02201_s01.do.

43. NBC News, "NBC News Special."

44. "In the nonviolent movement everyone can be a participant," Lawson later explained. "What is so important is the vitality of your character, your courage, and your concern for the change that you want. That's what equalizes everybody, so that it's not a question of the survival of the fittest or those who are physically in the best condition. . . . Everyone can do the work." Lawson, "Interview: Rev. James Lawson."

45. Lawson, interview by Robert Penn Warren.

46. NBC News, "NBC News Special."

47. Lawson, "Interview: Rev. James Lawson."

48. The students had already been successful in using sit-ins to bring down "White" and "Colored" signs in the train and Greyhound bus stations in Nashville.

49. Lawson, "Interview: Rev. James Lawson."

50. Quoted in Ernest M. Limbo, "James Lawson: The Nashville Civil Rights Movement," in *The Human Tradition in the Civil Rights Movement*, ed. Susan M. Glisson (Lanham, MD: Roman and Littlefield, 2006), 176.

51. NBC News, "NBC News Special."

52. Jennifer Stollman, "Diane Nash: 'Courage Displaces Fear, Love Transforms Hate': Civil Rights Activism and the Commitment to Nonviolence," in *The Human Tradition in the Civil Rights Movement*, ed. Susan M. Glisson (Lanham, MD: Roman and Littlefield, 2006).

53. Quoted in Halberstam, *The Children*, 216.

54. Limbo, "James Lawson," 158.

55. For an account of the Freedom Rides compiled by those who participated, see "Freedom Rides of 1961," Veterans of the Civil Rights Movement website, http://www.crmvet.org/riders/freedom_rides.pdf.

56. Raymond Arsenault, *Freedom Riders: 1961 and the Struggle for Racial Justice* (New York: Oxford University Press, 2006), chap. 4; and Richard Weingroff, *The Road to Civil Rights*, Federal Highway Administration website, April 8, 2015, http://www.fhwa.dot.gov/highwayhistory/road/s27.cfm.

57. Arsenault, *Freedom Riders*, 181; Weingroff, *Road to Civil Rights*, 126.

58. James Lawson, "James Lawson: How the Nashville Movement Kept the Riders Riding," *Breach of Peace: Portraits of the 1961 Mississippi Freedom Riders,* website, July 25, 2008, http://breachofpeace.com/blog/?p=57.

59. Arsenault, *Freedom Riders*, 195.

60. Howard Zinn, *SNCC: The New Abolitionists* (Boston: Beacon Press, [1964]), 51.

61. Quoted in Arsenault, *Freedom Riders*, 262.

Dolores Huerta during the Gallo strike, 1973. *Courtesy of Walter P. Reuther Library, Archives of Labor and Urban Affairs, Wayne State University.*

CHAPTER 4

THE GRAPE BOYCOTT

Preeti Sharma, Mayra Jones, and Sophia Cheng

During the same decade that sit-ins and the Freedom Rides were making history in the South, a powerful coalition of workers, students, clergy, community organizations, and unions launched one of the most influential boycotts in US labor history. The campaign mobilized not only activists across the country but also millions of consumers who refused to buy California table grapes.[1] The activists embraced the theory and practice of nonviolence taught by Mohandas Gandhi and drew on lessons learned in earlier direct action campaigns. By focusing national and international attention on the injustice that workers faced in the fields, the boycott ultimately secured the unionization of thousands of farmworkers, improving wages and working conditions and altering public consciousness about the hands that feed us.

FOUNDING THE NFWA

In the 1950s profit in the US agriculture industry was realized through the exploitation of immigrants and people of color. Farmworkers throughout California's central valley spent hours each day in the harsh sun, repeatedly bending down to pick grapes, tomatoes, lettuce, celery, and other crops. They worked in dismal conditions, received poverty wages—workers were paid on average fifty to sixty cents an hour—and were exposed to unsafe pesticides while being denied benefits such as unemployment and health insurance, pensions, and vacations.[2] They were routinely deprived of "the right to have clean drinking water, access to portable toilets, lunch breaks, or short rest breaks."[3] Growers recruited a diverse population of workers, mostly Mexicans but also Filipino Americans and African Americans, creating competition between racial/ethnic groups and inhibiting collective action.

US labor laws in the 1950s provided virtually no protections for farmworkers. Between 1942 and 1964 the federal bracero program allowed labor contractors to recruit thousands of Mexican nationals as guest farmworkers. These laborers were denied permanent legal status, and many were deported at the end of their contract. In addition, agriculture and domestic employment—sectors in which workers of color were concentrated—were explicitly excluded from the National Labor Relations Act (NLRA) of

1935, which gave most workers the right to form and join unions, to engage in collective bargaining, and to participate in collective actions, including strikes. The law, designed to protect agricultural interests in the South, was exploited by growers in California.

The deplorable plight of the farmworkers motivated two charismatic Mexican American leaders, Dolores Huerta and César Chávez, to advance a vision for just and humane conditions in the fields. Huerta had met Chávez in 1956 at a fundraiser for the Community Service Organization (CSO), a civil rights organization and self-help association that provided services for working people across California and sought to build their civic power.

Although neither Huerta nor Chávez had organized farmworkers before they met, both had worked for the CSO during the early 1950s.[4] Coincidentally, both were drawn to the teachings of Gandhi. Huerta recalled, "When I had first met César Chávez, I did not know that he had read all about Gandhi as I had. We were both committed to the whole lifestyle of Gandhi—of voluntary poverty, of nonviolence, and also of sharing resources."[5]

Huerta and Chávez valued Gandhi's teachings as a way to understand community building, organizing, and resisting oppression. Huerta studied Gandhi because she was "always interested in organizing."[6] As a high school student she had read all she could about Gandhi. Gandhi had gained an international reputation through his campaign of nonviolent resistance against British rule in India, but Huerta connected with Gandhi's successful challenges to racism. "When you read Gandhi's story, and all the things that happened to him as an Indian and the way that he was treated, I just thought it was fascinating," she said. "It's a lot of the same things I went through."[7] To Huerta, nonviolence provided a way to challenge discrimination, institutional racism, and poverty. Chávez also had a deep admiration for Gandhi's practice of nonviolence as a movement for social change.[8]

> When we apply Gandhi's philosophy of nonviolence, it really forces us to think, really forces us to work hard. But it has power. It attracts the support of the people. I've learned that, if any movement is on the move, violence is the last thing wanted. Violence only seems necessary when people are desperate; frustration often leads to violence.[9]

Chávez's study of nonviolence taught him about power dynamics and the importance of disciplined reflection, work, and action.[10]

Although Chávez and Huerta began organizing farmworkers in different parts of California, they came together again in the early 1960s.[11] Chávez, who was concerned about the continuing violence directed against farmworkers at the hands of growers, went to Huerta's home and asked her to join the fight to unionize. Huerta recalled that Chávez said, "Farmworkers will never have a union unless you and I do it." "I thought he was joking," she continued, "but then he added, 'We will never see a national union of

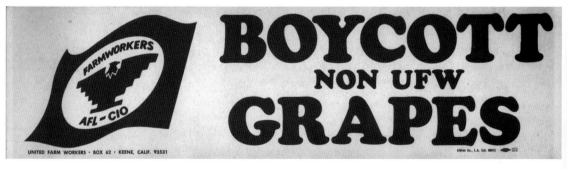

Grape boycott bumper sticker, ca. 1968.

César's dream was to have ashrams, like they did in India. **Everybody would live together**. People would work together. All of your resources were pooled, to **help the community grow**, to spread the whole idea of nonviolence.
　　—Dolores Huerta May 2013

farmworkers in our lifetime because the growers are too rich, powerful, and racist.'"[12] Huerta agreed, and in 1962 she and Chávez founded the National Farm Workers Association (NFWA) in Delano, California, and began to pursue the impossible dream. The NFWA held its first organizing convention in Fresno in September of that year, with 280 farmworkers from sixty-five farming communities attending as voting delegates. The participants ratified a constitution, voted the "Aztec thunderbird," or black eagle, as their emblem, and elected Chávez as the organization's president.[13] Huerta and Chávez agreed that the NFWA would embrace Gandhian nonviolence as its guiding philosophy as the organization fought to secure farmworkers' rights.[14]

THE DELANO GRAPE STRIKE

The NFWA's founders initially planned on launching a large-scale campaign against growers after building a membership base. "We said we would organize for five years and then do a general strike," Huerta recalled.[15] Utilizing the community organizing tactics they had learned through the CSO, Chávez drove across California, focusing full time on house visits, service provision, and advocacy, while Huerta concentrated on organizing activities in the evening, after her job with the CSO. To help build a membership base and to serve the community, the NFWA held clinics, prepared income taxes, helped with education concerns, and provided childcare. "We organized through families," Huerta said. "Before we even tried to organize a company, first we tried to organize a community."[16]

Another farmworkers' organization, the Agricultural Workers Organizing Committee (AWOC), was also organizing in California at that time. AWOC, which had been founded in 1959 and was affiliated with the AFL-CIO, was comprised largely of Filipino American farmworkers. Philip Vera Cruz and Larry Itliong were among the founders. Many of the workers, like Vera Cruz and Itliong, were labor veterans.[17]

In 1965 the AWOC launched a strike against the grape growers in Delano. Vera Cruz, who went on to become a UFW vice president, described the meeting that launched the strike.

> On September 8, 1965, at the Filipino Hall at 1457 Glenwood St. in Delano, the Filipino members of AWOC held a mass meeting to discuss and decide whether to go on strike or accept the reduced wages proposed by the growers. The decision was "to strike," and it became one of the most significant and famous decisions ever made in the entire history of the farmworkers' labor struggles in California.

It was like an incendiary bomb, exploding out the strike message to the workers in the vineyards, telling them to have sit-ins in the labor camps, and set up picket lines at every grower's ranch.[18]

Itliong asked the NFWA to join the action, telling Huerta, "We are going to have a strike meeting and I want you to come to be there with us." After discussing the request with Chávez, Huerta went to the meeting, "where they voted they were going to go on strike in Delano."[19]

Huerta and Chávez were concerned about the prospects for success in Delano. The AWOC had led a strike of grape pickers in the Coachella Valley the previous summer that had resulted in a wage increase, and the union hoped to repeat that victory. Conditions were different in Delano, however. In Coachella, the crops were smaller and most of the workers who had walked out were Filipino American. In contrast, the Delano workforce included Mexican, Chicano, Puerto Rican, and African American farmworkers as well. Given the large scale of the Delano fields and the diverse, multiracial workforce, Huerta and Chávez wondered whether joining the AWOC for the strike would be the best choice for the NFWA. The organizers did not know whether the action would be a short-term work stoppage or a long-term strike, and financing was a problem. "We only had about $70 in our bag," Huerta stated. "That's all the money we had."[20]

When the AWOC strikers faced violent retaliation from the growers, support for the strike solidified. "The Filipino workers were attacked," Huerta recalled. "Some of them were beaten up. They lived in the labor camp and [the growers] had shut off the light, water, and gas so they couldn't even eat."[21] The NFWA called a meeting on September 16, 1965—Mexican Independence Day—and the membership voted to support the Filipino American farmworkers through a solidarity strike. The AWOC and the NFWA set up a joint strike committee, and the Delano grape strike began.[22]

The Delano grape strike became the longest strike in farm labor history.[23] Over the next five years the unions targeted powerful agricultural companies, including Schenley Industries, DiGiorgio Fruit Corporation, and Giumarra Vineyards Corporation. The strike evolved into a national boycott that transformed the power relationship between farmworkers and growers through nonviolent action, and it trained a new generation of organizers and activists.

MOVING FROM STRIKE TO BOYCOTT

The large number of farms and the distance between them posed challenges for maintaining the strike lines in Delano. The strikers set up a system of roving picket lines that traveled from farm to farm. The AWOC and the NFWA had initially decided to split the farms between them, but the picketers ended up working together.[24] Growers sought court injunctions against the strike and called in local law enforcement to arrest striking workers. The strikers embraced the philosophy of nonviolence even though they encountered violence from the growers and law enforcement alike. The growers' foremen patrolled the ranch properties armed with shotguns, and the growers hired armed security guards who would routinely threaten and brutalize workers. The violent repression of the strikers and an influx of strikebreakers compelled organizers to reach out for help. Chávez and Huerta traveled to college campuses in the San Francisco Bay Area and Los Angeles to recruit supporters for the strike. Students as well as clergy joined the action, and they too experienced violence on the picket lines.

Few members of the NFWA had ever participated in a strike, and facing emotional and physical assault on the picket lines took its toll.[25] Chávez decided to recruit seasoned youth activists from the desegregation movement in the South, including

Labor activists involved in the planning of the Paolo Agbayani Retirement Village for elderly Filipino farmworkers gather for a photograph in October 1972. Among them is Philip Vera Cruz (back row, fifth from the right). The facility, part of the UFW's Forty Acres complex in Delano, California, opened in 1975. *Courtesy of Walter P. Reuther Library, Archives of Labor and Urban Affairs, Wayne State University.*

members of the Congress of Racial Equality (CORE) and the Student Nonviolent Coordinating Committee (SNCC), to train the Delano strikers. The training included "dealing with the police, maintaining discipline, devising creative alternatives, and resisting grower provo-cations."[26] The nonviolence training fostered connections between the desegregation activists and the farmworkers. Activists like Mike Miller and Marshall Ganz and staff from the new SNCC newspaper, *The Movement*, became key supporters of the strike. In October the SNCC shipped radios from Georgia to Delano to help the striking workers communicate across the 1,000-square-mile area in which the farms were located.[27] The arrival of the desegregation leaders from the SNCC and CORE also brought greater public attention to the picket lines, which likely reduced violence. Chávez noted to a reporter that police were "not even using dogs" and related that he had overheard a police officer commenting, "We don't want another Selma here."[28]

As winter approached, the industry-wide impact of the strike began to diminish, and the NFWA needed to reconsider striking as its core tactic. Huerta acknowledged that the growers were wearing down the union members.

> Every time we pull crews out [of jail], [the growers] bring in more strikebreakers. Because we are so close to Mexico, they could just go down there in four hours and bring people back. So it was obvious we are not going to win this strike, although we did make a big dent.[29]

Huerta contacted Stewart Weinberg, a civil rights attorney from San Francisco, for advice. He told her about CORE's boycott of auto dealerships in San Francisco that had denied employment to African Americans. "So Stew Weinberg says, 'Have you guys thought about doing a boycott?' Like CORE was doing," recalled Huerta. "We said, 'Okay, why don't we try that.'"[30]

In December 1965 the NFWA launched a boycott against Schenley.[31] The NFWA chose Schenley because the company was not only a California grower but also a wine and liquor company. It distributed wine made from Delano grapes and recognizable brands, like Cutty Sark scotch whiskey, that consumers could easily identify and refuse to purchase.[32] Schenley products were well known on the East Coast. The strike had developed leadership among the workers and had exposed the brutality of the growers, but a national boycott could have greater impact by placing economic pressure on the growers. Chávez likened the boycott to an everyday democratic process:

> The boycott is a way to vote at the marketplace, which is a lot more powerful than going through politicians. When you go to the marketplace, you by-pass all of the politicians, all the public policy machine, and you can get a reaction. Instead of voting once every four years, you can vote every day in the market-place. The polls never close and you don't need a majority to win. More people need to know that. The boycott is a very powerful tool.[33]

The boycott represented an innovative strategy for the NFWA. It mobilized supporters outside the labor community in direct action and creative nonviolent resistance by engaging consumers to challenge the economic power of the growers. It also increased the public's awareness of the conditions of workers in the fields through the use of slogans such as "There's blood on those grapes."

In New York the farmworkers found solidarity with the SNCC and CORE. Both organizations held meetings to plan boycott actions, launched letter writing campaigns, coordinated picket lines at grocery stores in New York and New Jersey, and visited liquor stores, where delegations asked managers to remove Schenley products and to display pro-union boycott posters. If the liquor stores did not comply, volunteers would set up a picket line. This campaign succeeded in persuading twenty liquor stores in Brooklyn and forty-nine liquor stores in Harlem to stop selling Schenley products.[34]

In 1966 the NFWA launched a highly publicized pilgrimage, or *peregrinación*, from Delano to Sacramento. Led by Chávez, a group of about seventy started the 340-mile journey from union headquarters to the steps of the state capitol on March 17. As they walked they were joined by farmworkers, community supporters, clergy, and students. The number of marchers had grown by hundreds when the pilgrimage reached Sacramento, and thousands joined the rally at the capitol on Easter Sunday, April 10. During the pilgrimage Chávez learned that Schenley had agreed to recognize the NFWA and to sign a contract. Within four months of the start of the Schenley boycott, the company had come to the bargaining table and recognized the union.

While union members and their supporters celebrated the landmark victory for farmworkers, the NFWA's leaders wasted no time before applying "a weapon that was proving highly effective" to a new target—DiGiorgio Fruit Corporation, one of California's largest growers and the producer of TreeSweet juices and S&W canned foods.[35] Huerta remembered that "as soon as Schenley recognized us on the way to the capitol (Sacramento), everybody made new signs, 'Boycott S&W products.'"[36] NFWA leaders met with DiGiorgio after Schenley recognized the union, hoping that DiGiorgio would follow suit and negotiate a contract. During the negotiations DiGiorgio guards violently threatened a woman organizer and physically attacked a male union supporter at the company's Delano vineyard.[37] The NFWA announced its boycott strategy against DiGiorgio in mid-April 1966.

Farmworkers participating in a UFW strike in Coachella, 1970s. *Courtesy of Walter P. Reuther Library, Archives of Labor and Urban Affairs, Wayne State University.*

In August 1966 the NFWA and the AWOC officially merged as the United Farm Workers Organizing Committee (UFWOC, or UFW).[38] Chávez was elected president, and Huerta, Itliong, and Vera Cruz were elected to the founding board of directors.

EXPANDING THE BOYCOTT NATIONWIDE

Di Giorgio signed a union contract in 1967, and Guimarra Vineyards became the next target. The boycott against Guimarra began that September. Guimarra shipped its grapes under hundreds of different labels, which caused confusion and made the boycott more difficult. The UFW decided to commence an industry-wide grape boycott that would urge consumers to stop buying and eating all nonunion California table grapes. When asked if the Schenley boycott had been planned as a stepping-stone to a national boycott of all table grapes, Huerta explained, "It was to get Schenley to the bargaining table." The scale of the boycott had grown much larger than had been originally intended.[39]

The UFW announced the nationwide boycott in July 1968.[40] This was a secondary boycott since it was directed against distributors and retailers, not just the employers of the striking workers. Although the 1947 Taft-Hartley Act barred most unions from organizing secondary boycotts, the UFW was not covered by it or the National Labor Relations Act. This allowed the UFW to boycott not only grapes but also the stores that sold the grapes. *The Movement* captured this irony in an article about the 1966 boycott.

Its worst handicap has been turned into one of its best assets. . . . It cannot appeal to the National Labor Relations Board to force the growers to sign a contract. But it also means that the crippling secondary boycott laws do not necessarily apply to the NFWA. . . . It has been given the freedom and mobility of a people's movement.[41]

The aim of the national boycott was to appeal to the conscience of consumers, who could disrupt ties between grape growers and their major distributors, the grocery stores, by refusing to purchase grapes. Huerta recalled that the union had to rely on union supporters and consumers to take action themselves. "The growers sued all the unions for millions of dollars, then we had to depend on people."[42] The national boycott received widespread support from unions, students, clergy, community and women's organizations, and members of the general public.

The UFW organized boycott offices in cities across the nation and initiated campaigns to pressure small grocery stores to stop buying California table grapes. After achieving success with small independent stores, the campaign expanded, exerting pressure on supermarket chains, including A&P and Safeway. In cities throughout the country, community supporters and students targeted grocery stores. They would organize a delegation to meet with the store management, and the delegation would ask store managers to stop buying California table grapes. If the management refused, the supporters would set up picket lines and ask consumers to not patronize the market until the management agreed to stop buying grapes. Consumers also staged creative actions called "shop-ins," which were reminiscent of the Nashville sit-ins. Huerta said that

> students would come in droves and do shop-ins. They would get their shopping carts and put all kinds of stuff, frozen food at the bottom. Then little things— spices and things of that nature, and pile them on top. Then, when they would get to the checkout counter, [they would] say, "Do you have union grapes here?" They would just leave the shopping cart there, and they would take off.[43]

These tactics, employed inside and outside of the stores, disrupted business and cut into profits.

In addition to pressuring supermarkets to stop stocking grapes, the UFW worked with unions to halt their distribution and sale, as Huerta noted.

> In 1968 we got all of the labor unions to support us. The longshoremen's union wouldn't hold the grapes. The retail clerks wouldn't put the grapes on the shelves. The railroad car workers . . . would let people know when the grapes were coming. The meat cutters had merged with the UFCW [United Food and Commercial Workers] and had very strong support of the grape boycott. In New York City, they took all the grapes out.[44]

The solidarity was so strong between the unions and the farmworkers that the boycott spread overseas. In February 1969 British dockworkers refused to unload California grapes.[45]

A critical element to the success of the boycott was the leadership of striking farmworkers who traveled from the fields to the cities to share their personal stories. The UFW dispatched strikers and their families from Central California to large cities. Some would carpool, while others would take a bus or hitchhike. "Once they would get to a city, they would go talk to the churches, labor organizations, community organizations, schools, and they would recruit people in those areas to do the boycott," Huerta recalled.[46] Huerta went to New York with several farmworkers who became organizers. The number of cities with

UFW boycott organizers and supporters grew, so the union created "boycott houses" in forty to fifty cities to provide accommodations. These accommodations were frequently arranged by churches or community groups.[47]

The campaign required a huge staff and thousands of supporters. Volunteers were needed at supermarkets in forty to fifty cities across the United States and Canada. Other volunteers were needed to continue to enlist community support from religious, student, labor, and community organizations. To recruit students, Huerta, Chávez, Vera Cruz, and other UFW leaders traveled to college campuses, where they asked students to support the grape boycott. College students would sign up at an event or presentation and then would be contacted by UFW staff within a day or two. Some students were recruited as boycott organizers. They would be assigned to a specific city and offered five dollars a week plus room and board. Huerta recalled that the union depended on committed student activists who joined the UFW boycott for no money, just food.[48]

Lilli Sprintz related that she urgently wanted to join the boycott after hearing about it at a grocery store in Philadelphia. Galvanized by the indignities that women farmworkers faced in the fields, she met with a UFW organizer, joined the campaign, and ended up working for the UFW for the next five years. Another college student, Harriet Teller, participated in a summer internship with the UFW while she was attending the University of Michigan. Teller was so moved by the eventual victory in 1970 that she left college and moved to St. Louis to work on a subsequent nonviolent boycott campaign for eighteen months.[49]

Clergy were an important source of moral support for the cause. Clergy and laity invited UFW leaders to speak at their worship services, signed on to support the boycott, and volunteered their time and money.[50] A local or national church endorsement made it socially acceptable for members of the congregation to express their solidarity as part of their religious beliefs. Activist Randy Shaw wrote that "once boycott volunteers, some of them active church members themselves, publicized the endorsement of local churches, people were much more willing to talk to them and to support the UFW campaign by not purchasing grapes."[51]

Lawson heard news reports about the grape boycott while he was a pastor in Memphis, and he began walking the picket lines at his local grocery store shortly after the Memphis sanitation strike concluded. Like other members of the clergy, he urged his one-thousand-member congregation at the Centenary United Methodist Church to stop buying table grapes and to join the picket line.[52] Memphis sanitation workers had fought against racial injustice and exploitation and succeeded in winning union recognition and a contract, so they felt a connection to the California farmworkers' movement.

Huerta also noted the important contributions of housewives and youth: "[We] had housewives. We [also] went to churches and got church people. We had junior high kids, high school kids, who would do press conferences. Everyone was talking about the farmworkers and how they were treated and ask[ing the public] to boycott."[53]

The participation of women volunteers was integral to the day-to-day work of the boycott. The UFW had hoped that using women as boycott leaders would minimize the use of violence, but Huerta noted that women and children were sometimes among the first to be hurt when picket lines were attacked.

> We had a situations where we put the women in the front, and [grocery market staff] would hit the women with their [metal] dollies. . . . The women would stand there and take it and the [market staff] couldn't do it much longer. The person hitting those young women on the shin couldn't keep it up. They had to stop. We had a lot of situations like that, where people were attacked because they were picketing and the idea was not to respond. It was really hard.[54]

Farmworkers, especially younger workers, were integral to the expansion of the boycott. They recruited and mobilized volunteers to support the boycott and staff the picket lines while sharing their firsthand experiences as farmworkers and strikers. One young farmworker named Jessica Govea had toiled in the fields with her family since the age of four. As a teenager she began helping the NFWA with clerical work; as a young adult she became the boycott coordinator for all of Canada, expanding the boycott beyond the United States. Govea went on to become a nationally recognized union leader and labor educator at Rutgers University and Cornell University.[55]

Eliseo Medina, who had never been outside Delano, recalled being asked to go to Chicago by Huerta and Chávez. He assumed Chicago was a short distance from home and at first was unaware that he would have to travel by plane.[56] Medina was instrumental in blocking grape distribution in the Midwest. In the late 1990s he became executive vice president of the Service Employees International Union, one of the largest unions in the country.

Miguel Contreras was a young farmworker from Dinuba, California, when he and his family of farmworkers were all fired for their participation with the UFW. Huerta recruited Contreras to launch a boycott in Toronto, Canada. Like other boycott leaders, he was paid five dollars a week, plus room and board at a Jesuit seminary.[57] The boycott changed his life. Contreras reflected, "I learned about courage and self-worth. Neither my father nor César Chávez thought of themselves or us as growers did . . . as nothing more than agricultural implements, to be used and discarded like you would discard an old shovel or an old hoe."[58] After his boycott experience with the farmworkers, Contreras worked as the national organizer for the Hotel Employees and Restaurant Employees Union, and in 1996 he was elected executive secretary-treasurer of the Los Angeles County Federation of Labor. He was the first Latino to lead the Los Angeles labor movement, and he successfully integrated the lessons from the UFW to build one of the most dynamic central labor councils in the country.

The boycott also drew from the energy of the diverse social movements of the late 1960s. In fact, Huerta recalled that the Black Panthers were among one of the first groups to endorse the boycott.

> You had people from Students for a Democratic Society, like Tom Hayden, talking about getting people to resist the war. You had the women's movement that was being formed. I was there with Gloria Steinem on many occasions, talking to women's organizations about supporting the grape boycott. A lot of people [were] going out there and speaking [about the boycott]. We would go to a city, we would get volunteers, and they would also go out to different places and then ask people to boycott.[59]

Boycott coordinators in each city sought support wherever they could find it. The social movements of the 1960s provided a rich source of student and community activists who wanted to get involved.

In a span of four years, the influence of the boycott had reached national and international proportions. On July 4, 1969, Chávez appeared on the cover of *Time* magazine, which ran a six-page article titled "The Little Strike That Grew to La Causa." The article opened with five everyday scenarios that reflected the grape boycott: guests at a dinner party who refuse the grapes offered by the host, students at a prep school who leave grapes untouched, customers at a grocery store who come in only to buy grapes, a housewife who apologizes for including grapes in a popular dessert, and a conservative youth group that organizes an "emergency grape lift" to fly grapes into Honolulu. The article explained the controversy surrounding the "smooth, sweet, and innocent fruit" and revealed the extent to which the grape boycott had influenced the national awareness of farmworkers and their movement.

> The welfare of agricultural workers has rarely captured US attention in the past, but the grape strike—*la huelga*—and the boycott accompanying it have clearly engaged a large part of the nation. The issue has divided husband and wife, inspired countless heated arguments at social occasions and engendered public controversy from coast to coast.[60]

The grape boycott became a household topic of debate and conversation. Millions of consumers were impacted by the boycott, and the massive public support ultimately pressured elected officials, policy makers, and growers to address the demands for justice by the farmworkers. The grape boycott attained such public prominence that the UFW declared May 30, 1969, "International Boycott Day." The event was marked with marches, vigils, parades, and picket lines throughout California and across the United States.[61]

A young Miguel Contreras holds a UFW flag, mid-1970s. *Courtesy of the Los Angeles County Federation of Labor.*

César Chávez breaks a twenty-five-day fast and accepts bread from Senator Robert Kennedy on March 10, 1968, in Delano, California. With them is Chávez's wife, Helen. *Photograph by Richard Darby. Courtesy of Walter P. Reuther Library, Archives of Labor and Urban Affairs, Wayne State University.*

After a five-year strike, John Guimarra signs the first contract between grape growers and the United Farm Workers. *Photograph by Cris Sanchez. Courtesy of Walter P. Reuther Library, Archives of Labor and Urban Affairs, Wayne State University.*

The boycott decreased sales of grapes by 12 percent nationally and in some major cities by more than 50 percent. In fact, it is estimated that about 17 million Americans, or 10 percent of the population, did not eat or buy grapes from 1966 to 1972.[62]

On July 28, 1970, Giumarra agreed to sign with the UFW, bringing one of the largest growers to the table. The next day two hundred farmworkers gathered in the Delano hiring hall to hear Chávez announce the victory. Huerta and Chávez were in the front line of the contract negotiations, which secured a three-year contract with the growers. The power of the UFW had grown from a few contracts representing 3,000 workers to over 200 contracts representing 70,000 workers.[63]

Throughout the grape strike and consumer boycott, the UFW continually recommitted itself to nonviolent struggle. The boycott emerged as one of the most powerful and memorable nonviolent campaigns to raise consciousness about the lives of farmworkers and to challenge injustice in the agricultural industry.

The UFW continued to rely on nonviolence as other consumer boycotts followed, including another grape boycott in the mid-1970s, a lettuce boycott, and a boycott of wine produced by California vintner Gallo. The story of California farmworkers was embraced as a national and international struggle. Farmworkers, students, clergy, labor, and community members forged a broad-based coalition and successfully mobilized millions to support the grape boycott. The legacy of the boycott lives on in the thousands of activists who were recruited and trained for labor and social justice movements, and in the millions of people who came to respect the power of the nonviolent boycott to advance the fight for human dignity.

NOTES

This chapter draws extensively from interviews of Rev. Lawson and guest speakers that were held during a special topics course sponsored by the Labor Center, the César E. Chávez Department of Chicana/o Studies, the Labor and Workplace Studies Minor, the Department of African American Studies, and the History Department at UCLA.

1. Randy Shaw, *Beyond the Fields: Cesar Chavez, the UFW, and the Struggle for Justice in the 21st Century* (Berkeley: University of California Press, 2008), 46.

2. Frank Bardacke, "Book Talk: Trampling Out the Vintage" (lecture, UCLA Institute for Research on Labor and Employment, Los Angeles, May 8, 2013); and Dolores Huerta, interview by Preeti Sharma, Mayra Jones, and Sophia Cheng, May 22, 2013, Los Angeles.

3. Susan Ferriss and Ricardo Sandoval, *The Fight in the Fields: Cesar Chavez and the Farmworkers Movement*, ed. Diana Hembree (New York: Harcourt Brace, 1997), 4.

4. Founded in 1947, the CSO was a civil rights organization and self-help association that provided services for and sought to build the civic power of working people in California. The organization focused on voter registration, lobbying, and citizenship classes. Huerta's father had been a farmworker in Mexico and California, and Chávez had been a farmworker in Arizona and California.

5. Huerta, interview by Sharma, Jones, and Cheng.

6. Ibid.

7. Ibid.

8. Winthrop Yinger, *Cesar Chavez: The Rhetoric of Nonviolence* (Pompano Beach: Exposition Press of Florida, 1975), 21.

9. Quoted in Frederick Dalton, *The Moral Vision of César Chávez* (New York: Orbis Books, 2003), 139. Chávez was introduced to Gandhi's biography by local clergy when he was organizing laborers in the Sal Si Puedes barrio of San Jose, California.

10. Dalton, *Moral Vision of César Chávez*, 138.

11. For a detailed discussion on the organizing leading up to the NFWA, see Ferriss and Sandoval, *Fight in the Fields*; Bardacke, "Book Talk"; Shaw, *Beyond the Fields*; and Craig Scharlin and Lilia

Villanueva, *Philip Vera Cruz: A Personal History of Filipino Immigrants and the Farmworkers Movement* (Washington: University of Washington Press, 2000).

12. Huerta, interview by Sharma, Jones, and Cheng.

13. Yinger, *Cesar Chavez*, 92.

14. Robin S. Doak, *Dolores Huerta: Labor Leader and Civil Rights Activist* (Minneapolis: Compass Point Books, 2008), 36.

15. Huerta, interview by Sharma, Jones, and Cheng.

16. Ibid.

17. Itliong had been a part of the strike against asparagus growers in the Stockton, California, area in 1948 and a shop steward with the International Longshore and Warehouse Union (ILWU) in Seattle, and he had held leadership positions with various Filipino community, labor, and voting rights organizations in Stockton. Vera Cruz was president of the local National Farm Labor Union (NFLU). For more information, see Dawn Mabalon, *Little Manila Is In the Heart* (Durham: Duke University Press, 2013), 259; and Scharlin and Villanueva, *Philip Vera Cruz*, 33–44, 48.

18. Quoted in Scharlin and Villanueva, *Philip Vera Cruz*, 35.

19. Huerta, interview by Sharma, Jones, and Cheng.

20. Ibid.

21. Ibid.

22. Ibid.

23. Yinger, *Cesar Chavez*, 92.

24. Frank Bardacke describes the relationship that formed between Mexican and Filipino American farmworkers through the beginnings of the AWOC and NFWA strike. Frank Bardacke, *Trampling Out the Vintage: Cesar Chavez and the Two Souls of the United Farm Workers* (New York: Verso Books, 2011), chap. 10.

25. Chavez told a reporter for *The Movement* that "over 90 percent of the strikers . . . have never been on strike before." "Strike in the Grapes!," in *The Movement 1964–1970*, ed. Clayborne Carson (Westport, CT: Greenwood Press, 1993), 71.

26. Marshall Ganz, *Why David Sometimes Wins: Leadership, Organization, and Strategy in the California Farm Worker Movement* (New York: Oxford University Press, 2010), 134.

27. "SNCC Radios Go to CORE, Delano Strike," in Carson, *The Movement*, 85.

28. "Harassment by Growers, Police," in Carson, *The Movement*, 72.

29. Huerta, interview by Sharma, Jones, and Cheng.

30. Ibid. Shaw, in *Beyond the Fields*, also points to the IWLU's spontaeous blocking of a docking ship with grapes in Oakland as another origin of the boycott (19). Lauren Araiza points to the boycott as stemming from civil rights strategies. Lauren Araiza, "Complicating the Beloved Community: The Student Nonviolent Coordinating Committee and the National Farm Worker Association," in *The Struggle in Black and Brown: African American and Mexican American Relations During the Civil Rights Era,* ed. Brian Benken (Lincoln: University of Nebraska Press, 2011), 87–88.

31. Yinger, *Cesar Chavez*, 93; and Huerta, interview by Sharma, Jones, and Cheng.

32. Araiza, "Complicating the Beloved Community," 88.

33. Quoted in Dalton, *Moral Vision of César Chávez*, 138–39. Chavez also said of the boycott picket line that a "supermarket boycott is an effective nonviolent weapon. Fire is not. When a fire destroys a supermarket, the company collects the insurance and rebuilds the store bigger and better, and also marks off the loss on its income tax. But picket lines take away customers and reduce business, and there is no way for the store to compensate for that. It is driven by sheer economics to want to avoid picket lines" (139).

34. Araiza, "Complicating the Beloved Community," 89.

35. Ferriss and Sandoval, *Fight in the Fields,* 126.

36. Huerta, interview by Sharma, Jones, and Cheng.

37. DiGiorgio's negative labor relations were so infamous and notorious that John Steinbeck used the company as a model to write *The Grapes of Wrath*.

38. United Farm Workers Organizing Committee changed its name to United Farm Workers (UFW) in 1972, after it became a full member of the AFL-CIO.

39. Huerta, interview by Sharma, Jones, and Cheng.

40. Yinger, *Cesar Chavez*, 96.

41. "How the Grapes Were Turned Back at the Docks," in Carson, *The Movement*, 95.

42. Huerta, interview by Sharma, Jones, and Cheng.

43. Ibid. In addition, Los Angeles had a "sip-ins" at wine tasting rooms. See Ganz, *Why David Sometimes Wins*, 222.

44. Huerta, interview by Sharma, Jones, and Cheng.

45. Yinger, *Cesar Chavez*, 97.

46. Huerta, interview by Sharma, Jones, and Cheng.

47. Shaw, *Beyond the Fields*, 40.

48. Huerta, interview by Sharma, Jones, and Cheng.

49. Shaw, *Beyond the Fields*, 24–25.

50. Marco G. Prouty, *César Chávez, the Catholic Bishops, and the Farmworkers' Struggle for Social Justice* (Tucson: University of Arizona Press, 2006), 28.

51. Shaw, *Beyond the Fields*, 37.

52. James Lawson, interview by Preeti Sharma and Ana Luz González, September 30, 2014, Los Angeles.

53. Huerta, interview by Sharma, Jones, and Cheng.

54. Ibid.

55. Shaw, *Beyond the Fields*, 30–31. For more on Jessica Govea, see Margaret Rose, "Women in the United Farm Workers: A Study of Chicana and Mexicana Participation in a Labor Union, 1950–1980" (PhD diss., University of California, Los Angeles, 1988), chap. 5.

56. Shaw, *Beyond the Fields*, 23.

57. Contreras went to Toronto in 1973. Kent Wong and Michael Viola, *Miguel Contreras: Legacy of a Labor Leader* (Los Angeles: UCLA Institute for Research on Labor and Employment, 2009).

58. Quoted in ibid., 8.

59. Huerta, interview by Sharma, Jones, and Cheng.

60. "The Little Strike that Grew to La Causa," *Time*, July 4, 1969, 16.

61. Yinger, *Cesar Chavez*, 99.

62. Shaw, *Beyond the Fields*, 46.

63. Ibid., 46.

Maria Elena Durazo at a protest against the New Otani Hotel in Los Angeles, 1996. *Courtesy of HERE Local 11.*

CHAPTER 5

HOTEL WORKERS TRANSFORM THE LABOR MOVEMENT

Caitlin Parker

In the 1990s an organizing revolution reshaped the labor movement in Los Angeles and across the nation. Backed by a largely immigrant Latino workforce, the president of the Hotel Employees and Restaurant Employees International Union (HERE) Local 11, Maria Elena Durazo, created a movement that empowered workers to fight for economic and social justice. Local 11's previous leadership, which was mostly male and white, had bargained with employers over wages and benefits with virtually no participation from the union's rank and file. Even though union membership was declining, these officials made no effort to organize the growing number of immigrant workers, assuming that they feared arrest or deportation and were willing to work for low wages. Under Durazo's leadership, Local 11 transformed itself by focusing on immigrant workers not just in the workplace, but by reaching out to the workers in the communities in which they lived.

Durazo drew inspiration from the civil rights and farmworkers' movements, calling on Rev. James M. Lawson Jr. and César Chávez to share their knowledge of nonviolent organizing. Through training in the strategy and tactics of nonviolence, the members of Local 11 developed the courage to risk their jobs, commit civil disobedience, and face possible arrest or deportation. Local 11 demanded justice for workers by engaging in various forms of direct action, including picket lines, street theater, hunger strikes, and media events. Workers became leaders in their own right as they shared stories of exploitation and resistance to recruit coworkers and community members to the cause. By the time Local 11 won its first major campaign against the Hyatt hotel chain in 1993, the union had proved the power of an organized immigrant workforce trained to use nonviolence to promote their cause. Local 11's example propelled progressive forces in the labor movement nationally and demonstrated how unions could lead the political fight for economic justice and immigrant rights.

The transformation of Local 11 can be traced through three pivotal campaigns. First, Local 11 developed a community-organizing model to challenge the labor practices of three Los Angeles Hyatt hotels from 1989 to 1991. Despite fears of retribution, workers learned to mobilize support in communities outside the workplace and to pressure the public and even the police to recognize workers' humanity through creative acts of nonviolence. Local 11 then solidified its community-labor coalition in a campaign against outsourcing at the University of Southern California (USC). The third campaign was for a living wage ordinance in Los Angeles, which the city council enacted in March 1997. It marked Local 11's first citywide legislative victory and helped to spark a nationwide movement for fair wages.

DURAZO'S EMERGENCE AS A LABOR LEADER

Durazo grew up as the daughter of immigrant farmworkers, and she understood the meaning of hard work. She and her family moved throughout California and Oregon, picking crops to support themselves. She experienced poverty and exploitation from a young age, learning firsthand about the abuse that workers face. She had her first experience with activism in 1970, when her older brother took her to the Chicano Moratorium in Fresno. Durazo marched alongside her mother and brother, arms locked, to protest the Vietnam War. Durazo's brother had burned his draft card and dedicated his life to organizing for the antiwar movement. "By engaging in marches and demonstrations in a nonviolent way, he personified what was being talked about in the civil rights movement in the South to me," Durazo said.[1] Inspired by her brother, Durazo became involved in activism at Saint Mary's College of California in Moraga. She committed her first act of civil disobedience as a sophomore, when she and classmates occupied the campus chapel to protest the school's failure to recruit and support Chicano students.

After graduating from college, Durazo organized with the Center for Autonomous Social Action (CASA) and the International Ladies' Garment Workers Union (ILGWU), which were connecting labor organizing to the fight for immigrant rights. Durazo joined CASA after meeting activist Humberto "Bert" Corona, who was organizing Mexican Americans and the immigrant community to fight for access to education, health care, and decent wages. Corona's effort to merge labor organizing and immigrant activism inspired Durazo. "It struck me that here we had the opportunity to do two things," she said. "We didn't want to just fight on the racial front [against] the discrimination in education and employment, all kinds of various discrimination. But, wow, there was actually a way to get power for workers."[2] Durazo became an organizer with ILGWU in 1979, after moving to Los Angeles. The ILGWU, one of the few unions that were organizing immigrant workers, had filed lawsuits against the US Immigration and Naturalization Service (INS) for entering workplaces without a warrant and rounding up workers without documents. Durazo's experiences with CASA and ILGWU taught her that an immigrant workforce can have power when the fight for immigrant rights is merged with the fight for labor rights.

After earning a law degree at People's College of Law in Los Angeles, Durazo began working at the labor law firm of Levy and Goldman, where she handed cases for HERE Local 11. She quickly realized that she missed organizing, which she has called "the love of my life."[3] In 1983 she was offered a job as an organizer for the local, and she eagerly accepted. Durazo quickly became aware of the many ways in which the local's white male leadership prevented the predominately immigrant workforce from gaining power. The longtime Local 11 president, Andrew "Scotty" Allan, refused to translate meetings, organizational materials, and contracts even though three-quarters of the membership spoke Spanish. The union office's hours of operation made it inaccessible to many workers. Hotel cleaners, for example, could not visit the union office after work because it closed at four o'clock in the afternoon.[4] Durazo tried to work around these limitations, but she found that her efforts were being undermined by the local's leadership. "I tried and I tried to organize as one organizer going into hotel after hotel, and gradually realized that this was not going to work," Durazo said. "You can't make change with your whole institution going in the opposite direction."[5] Union officials eventually fired her for disrupting the status quo.

Soon after she was fired, Durazo began to consider a challenge to Local 11's leadership. At first she was reluctant to run for president because she preferred organizing behind the scenes, but hotel workers and leaders in the labor movement encouraged her to campaign for the position. In 1987 Durazo led an insurgent slate of union members to oppose the incumbent leadership. A rival group disputed the election process and called for the national leadership of HERE to intervene. National officials placed Local 11 in trusteeship, suspending the local's bylaws, and sent in national union representatives Miguel Contreras, Bill Granfield, and Herman Leavitt to assume control.

The incumbent leadership of Local 11 had hoped that the trusteeship would stabilize the status quo, but Contreras, Granfield, and Leavitt came from the progressive wing of HERE, which was fighting similar battles with union officials at the national level. Durazo soon realized that the trustees shared her vision of nonviolent organizing and worker empowerment.

> My position was, whoa, you're coming in to control us, but we want transparency, we want resources for union organizing. We want to activate the members. We want organizing campaigns because there are lots of hotels that are non-union where the standards are bad. So I kept putting things on the table, and they said, "Yes, yes, we believe in that too!"[6]

Contreras quickly became Durazo's ally in using the strategy and tactics of nonviolence to rebuild the union from the ground up. Durazo's Catholic upbringing and her parents' dedication to serving others had instilled in her a respect for nonviolent organizing. "I think it was just the values that I grew up with that reinforced in the political context that nonviolence was just much, much more powerful [than violence]," she said. Durazo had seen violence used in the labor movement and did not think it was effective, and she, like Contreras, took inspiration from the farmworkers' movement and the leadership of César Chávez and Dolores Huerta. Durazo pointed out that she and Contreras had similar backgrounds.

> Miguel had come out of the movement, too. His father and mom were farmworkers and they had all gone out on strike. They had all gone to jail probably eighteen, twenty times. They'd gone to jail with nuns and priests and other farmworkers. I think the combination of his experience and my personal experience led us [to nonviolence].[7]

Contreras and Durazo became partners in the struggle to transform the union. They also fell in love and later married.

In 1989 Durazo ran again and was elected president of the 12,000-member Local 11 with 85 percent of the vote.[8] The election of a Chicana activist backed by immigrant workers marked a turning point for the labor movement in Los Angeles. Durazo's success in unseating the union's entrenched white-male leadership inspired workers to see the potential of organizing. "Many of us come from countries where the powerful always have their way," union member Lourdes Portugal told the *Los Angeles Times* following the election. "Maria Elena has made us realize that we can take control and run things the way we want. Now we can speak up when there is an injustice. Maria Elena has instilled this in us."[9]

Organizer Wins Post of President

Latina Leads Takeover of Union From Anglo Males

By MARITA HERNANDEZ,
Times Staff Writer

When union organizer Maria Elena Durazo took a job with the hotel and restaurant workers union six years ago, she found a union at war with itself.

The long-entrenched Anglo administrators were so out of touch with their predominantly Latino rank-and-file membership that when the members asked for Spanish translation of union meetings, their leaders told them to "learn English." The open animosity between union members and officials bordered on "hatred," she said.

Durazo never doubted that she would eventually help oust the old guard, but said she did not imagine that the change would come so swiftly or that she would end up at
Please see UNION, Page 28

JAN SONNENMAIR
Maria Elena Durazo

This article, "Organizer Wins Post of President: Latina Leads Takeover of Union from Anglo Males," was written by Marita Hernandez and was published in the *Los Angeles Times* on May 6, 1989. *Courtesy of HERE Local 11.*

TAKING ON HYATT AND TRANSFORMING LOCAL 11

One of the first calls that Durazo made following her election was to Lawson, then the pastor of Holman United Methodist Church. Durazo asked for Lawson's help in building the hotel workers' movement through the use of nonviolence. Lawson held workshops in the philosophy and tactics of nonviolence with Durazo and the executive committee of Local 11. This training proved to be key to the success of Local 11's first campaign, which was against the Chicago-based Hyatt Corporation.

In 1989 Hyatt moved to change how employees could be scheduled at its three Los Angeles hotels. The corporation wanted managers to be able to require employees to work up to ten consecutive days with no overtime pay, which was prohibited by the corporation's contract with Local 11.[10] The proposal also threatened Local 11's agreement with twenty other hotels that were covered by a master contract. Under the master contract, Local 11 would have to extend any concessions made to non-signees like Hyatt to master-contract hotels.[11] Two months of negotiations between executives and union representatives deteriorated after Hyatt refused to revise the proposed ten-day workweek. Durazo knew that taking on a two-billion-dollar corporation like Hyatt would require an aggressive rank-and-file campaign, which would require a dramatic increase in membership. She reached out to Lawson for guidance.[12]

Lawson and Durazo first focused on addressing workers' fears. Workers who associated with union organizers or protested while on the job could be fired or arrested. This was a frightening prospect for workers who had few economic resources and who prided themselves on being responsible members of their community. Lawson recalled how potent that fear was.

Miguel Contreras and Maria Elena Durazo on a picket line in Los Angeles in the late 1980s. *Courtesy of HERE Local 11.*

[One] issue that came up was the abject fear as the hotels increased the supervision, increased the workloads. And we're talking about people who were making very low wages anyway. But they needed that work just to keep bread on the table. And so we did this business about not relying on the workplace for the major organizing, but going into the community where people lived.[13]

Since many workers were afraid to interact with union representatives at the workplace, Local 11 initiated home visits. The home visits became a critical element of Local 11's organizing strategy, as Durazo noted. *recruitment through home visits*

> The laws in this country do not protect workers when they speak up. And so we had to have those extensive conversations in their homes. And eventually we had to have it with the families, the spouses, the partners, the kids, because they were going to start spending more time to organize their co-workers. And so it became a community project where everyone was involved.[14]

As workers became organizers and recruited their colleagues through home visits, the ranks of Local 11 grew.

Many of Local 11's new organizers were unfamiliar with or resistant to nonviolent approaches. Lawson introduced the hotel workers to the philosophy of nonviolence and taught them how to respond to provocation. "Reverend Lawson put it all in context. . . . What it was like to get arrested, what it was like to get kicked, to get spit on, to get beat up," Durazo said. Lawson conducted role-playing exercises, similar to those he had created for the student sit-in campaigns of the civil rights movement, in which partners took turns practicing nonviolent resistance in the face of verbal and physical abuse. "You would get pushed, you would get shoved, you would get cussed at, and you were tested," Durazo explained.

> We did this internally with our staff. Now this is pretty much all Latinos, and mostly immigrants' first experience with a union, first experience with any kind of activism. And Reverend Lawson is teaching us about nonviolence and how to do that. . . . And it resonated. It really touched everyone in every single session. So that's where we became close friends, because of the transformation he helped me and others make in the culture of the union.[15]

Lawson's training sessions also gave workers the courage to face the police at demonstrations and assert their rights as workers. Lawson stressed the strategic value of not making the police the target. Instead, the goal was to strengthen the union. Local 11 protestors were taught to engage the police officers by explaining the aims of civil disobedience and to avoid confrontation. Engagement did not always preclude arrest, however, as Lawson noted. He was arrested more frequently with Local 11 than he had been during the civil rights protests of the 1950s and 1960s. At times Lawson and Durazo would continue strategizing as they were arrested and transported to local jails. Nonetheless, Local 11's efforts to interact with the Los Angeles Police Department ultimately contributed to the establishment of a labor liaison office.[16]

Lawson's training in nonviolent tactics, along with the growth in union membership that resulted from the home visits, allowed Local 11 to escalate its campaign against Hyatt. Drawing on the successful sit-in strategy that he had employed in Nashville in 1960, Lawson led union members in a series of sit-ins at the Hyatt Regency's restaurant. The restaurant was an ideal target because it was a popular lunch location for corporate executives. Union members and allies would occupy every table so that no customer could sit down. They ordered only water to deprive Hyatt of its lunchtime revenue while leaving tips for the waiters. These sit-ins, which came to be known as "water-ins" among the union

Lawson jailed more in LA than the South

Maria Elena Durazo speaks with police in Los Angeles, 1990s. *Courtesy of HERE Local 11.*

members, sent a powerful message to the corporation. Union members also held "wake-up calls" by banging drums outside the three Hyatt hotels at six thirty in the morning.[17]

By the third year of the campaign, many of the rank and file had begun to doubt Local 11's ability to overcome Hyatt's resistance. In May 1991 Hyatt pressured workers by weakening employee health benefits and refusing to restore them until the workers accepted the ten-day workweek.[18] Durazo could sense the momentum behind the daily struggle waning and decided that her campaign members needed a spiritual revitalization. In June Durazo invited Lawson and Chávez to join the workers at a rally in downtown Los Angeles. The event began with a march from the Hyatt Regency to the First United Methodist Church. At the church Chávez described his organizing experiences with farmworkers in the Central Valley. "Those who persist are those who win," Chávez told the workers at the rally. "The greatest fear the boss has is of your commitment. He is not afraid of money, bombs, bullets, or even power. It is the fear of the people, who, no matter how humble they are, commit themselves."[19] Lawson talked about the power of nonviolence in the civil rights movement. Durazo recalled that he "spoke in terms that connected with anybody, even across language, culture, and ethnicity."[20]

Placing the Hyatt fight in the context of the long history of nonviolent protest buoyed the spirits and resolve of the striking workers. Nonviolence provided "the spiritual sustenance we needed," Durazo reflected. "Because if it's a matter of, 'Okay, I want to make twenty-five cents more an hour, fifty cents more an hour,' people just don't sustain for those kinds of issues. They sustain because there's a bigger, moral issue. A bigger dignity issue."[21] The knowledge that they were struggling toward a common goal created a sense of collective responsibility among the workers. "Local 11 became a kind of community in which people relied upon one another. They worked with each other, they were empowered personally, they treated each other with decency," Lawson recalled. "There was a great sense in which the union became a kind of family."[22]

When national headquarters pledged to increase resources and supply staff for a national campaign, Hyatt capitulated at the bargaining table. HERE Local 11 signed a new contract with the three Los Angeles Hyatt hotels in November 1991. This victory reenergized the labor movement nationally. Local 11 had demonstrated how creative acts of nonviolence could disrupt the workplace and bring multibillion-dollar corporations back to the negotiating table. The key to the success of the Hyatt campaign was solidarity among the workers, not only those who worked at Hyatt hotels but also those at other hotels who took part in civil disobedience actions against Hyatt. Durazo described one of these workers to a reporter from the *Los Angeles Times*.

> One of our executive board members, Pearl Daniels, a sixty-year-old black woman, has gotten arrested several times, not for her own contract but to help brothers and sisters in other places win contracts. She had never done that before, until she got into an atmosphere of seeing that was the only way to win.[23]

EXPANDING THE TACTICS OF NONVIOLENT ORGANIZING

The Hyatt campaign transformed Local 11 by empowering workers to become leaders in the fight for economic justice. As they planned for subsequent campaigns in the hotel industry and throughout Los Angeles, organizers and workers focused on an important element of Lawson's first step for nonviolent organizing: the need for research to understand the power structures of the adversary.[24] Durazo stressed that research became an important part of launching any nonviolent campaign for Local 11.

> It used to be we'd have a dispute with a particular corporation, and we would go out on strike and see what happened. We're not going to do that anymore. We're going to find out what hurts that employer. We find out where they make their money and how they make their money, and we go to those points.[25]

HERE's national office provided information on corporate finances in the hotel industry that enabled workers to place their own experiences into a broader context of economic inequality and exploitation. Armed with this knowledge, workers could speak out against their employer while forging alliances with workers in other hotels and even other industries.

HERE Local 11 staged dramatic protests outside the workplace that were calculated to gain public support and embarrass abusive employers. In 1994 South Korean conglomerate Hanjin Group terminated 575 hotel workers at the Hilton hotel in downtown Los Angeles. In protest, Local 11 held a "hotel in the street," a demonstration used in several campaigns that called attention to the often invisible work of maids, cooks, dishwashers, and other service staff who cater behind the scenes to hotel guests. Local 11 set up beds outside the hotel, in the middle of a busy downtown intersection. Rose Rivera, a housekeeper, made the beds one by one while her co-worker Guadalupe Garcia narrated the housekeeper's story. "What would we do without our work? There's no one else to take care of my family," said Garcia, a widowed mother of three. After the performance, Garcia, Durazo, and more than thirty other workers were arrested and charged with unlawful assembly.[26] "Hotel in the street" demonstrated that "these jobs belong to the people who did the work, not the management company or the ownership," Durazo explained.

Members of Local 11 also forged alliances with the immigrant rights movement and local university, community, and religious groups.[27] Community alliances across race and ethnicity proved especially powerful in negotiating with foreign-owned companies. In 1992 the Koreana Hotel Co., a South Korean company, bought the Hyatt Wilshire Hotel, one of the hotels targeted in the 1989–91 Hyatt campaign, and terminated the contract that Local 11 workers had fought so hard to win.[28] Local 11 allied itself with the Asian Pacific American Labor Alliance (APALA) and Korean Immigrant Workers Advocates (KIWA) to picket the South Korean embassy and to lobby Koreana to reinstate the workers, which it ultimately did.[29] Likewise, the 1996 campaign against Japanese-owned New Otani Hotel gained support from the Little Tokyo People's Rights Organization (LTPRO), which had previously fought redevelopment and the displacement of community residents caused by the hotel. Asian American students from UCLA also organized with the union.[30]

Through research and organizing, Local 11 connected the plight of hotel workers to broader patterns of economic inequality in the city. In the spring of 1992, Local 11 released a video that highlighted how city government subsidized the tourism industry through its redevelopment policies. Titled *City on the Edge*, the video contrasted the city's public image of sunshine and glamour to the reality of poverty, violence, and economic inequality. Local 11 mailed the video to Mayor Tom Bradley, city officials, and an estimated 2,500 convention planners around the country. The video was criticized for undermining the city's tourism industry, which was facing serious losses following civil unrest in April 1992, but it offered a solution: to pay all the city's workers a living wage. The video concluded with this warning:

> As it moves towards becoming Los Angeles's largest employer, the tourism industry sets the pace for the city's economy. If the industry traps more of LA's workforce in permanent poverty, the city's image problem will also become permanent. But the tourism industry can choose to lead Los Angeles in a different direction. It can provide for its workforce and ensure tourism's growth at the same time. For now, LA remains a city on the edge.[31]

Leaders of the AFL-CIO, including Linda Chavez-Thompson, John Sweeney, Richard Trumka, and Maria Elena Durazo, lead a march during HERE Local 11's campaign against New Otani Hotel in 1996. *Courtesy of HERE Local 11.*

COMMUNITY COALITIONS IN THE USC CAMPAIGN

In 1996 Lawson, Durazo, and Local 11 expanded the union's community alliances in a campaign against the University of Southern California (USC), the largest private employer in Los Angeles. The campaign began when USC began to outsource work to subcontractors to avoid providing benefits and job security to its employees, most of whom lived in the neighborhoods surrounding the campus. Food service workers and janitors were faced with the option of either losing their jobs or entering a nonunion working agreement with lower wages and no healthcare benefits. Over three hundred cafeteria workers and janitors decided to take on the wealthy university. The campaign triggered a four-year battle to obtain a contract with protections against nonunion outsourcing.

When workers began to hold protests on the USC campus in the spring of 1996, the university administration sought to prevent them from organizing. USC obtained an injunction against HERE Local 11 that permitted only ten workers to assemble in the center of campus and only five workers to congregate at any campus building. Larger protests had to take place at least fifty feet away from campus entrances. When members of the USC Student Coalition Against Labor Exploitation (SCALE) tried to protest alongside workers, the administration attempted to place harsh restrictions on the student group's on-campus demonstrations as well. The campus United University Church offered the workers its parking lot as a space for demonstrations. Although the lot was within the boundaries of campus, it was church property and therefore exempt from the injunction.[32] Local 11 set up tents and trailers in the parking lot and used it as a base for public vigils, strikes, and a weeklong fast. Eventually, Durazo said, "there was so much pressure on—from the administration on the church—that they kicked us off. So we ended up going across the street."[33]

After the relocation Local 11 held a "rolling fast" that lasted five months. Fasting as a form of protest was familiar to many USC workers because they knew about the farmworkers' struggles for justice.[34] Community leaders, clergy, and elected officials supported the rolling fast by speaking out against the university's actions. Durazo spoke before the city council in May 1999, on the ninth day of her eleven-day hunger strike, calling her sacrifice "little compared to the daily sacrifices made by workers at USC and throughout Los Angeles." In response, four councilmembers visited the USC campus to lend support to the workers. One of the councilmembers, Joel Wachs, criticized the USC administration for claiming to need "flexibility" in hiring despite a $1.5 billion endowment. "If you look at what they pay some of these football and basketball coaches and compare that to what they pay the people who clean the auditoriums, it's ridiculous," Wachs stated. "A lot of this is about values."[35] When Durazo ended her hunger strike she passed on a wooden cross worn by César Chávez to Gilbert Cedillo, a state assembly member, who fasted for three days before passing the cross on to Contreras, now head of the Los Angeles County Federation of Labor. Actor Martin Sheen was the next in line. As the rolling fast continued, Lawson and other religious leaders held daily noontime services to bless those who were fasting and to lead the workers in prayer. Helen Chávez, widow of César Chávez, requested that a campus plaque honoring her husband be covered until the university came to a fair settlement with the workers.[36]

Creative acts of nonviolence sustained morale during the long struggle against USC, just as they had during the Hyatt campaign. One activist reported feeling "disillusioned and burned out on the labor movement" until he became involved in the USC campaign. "That was just really fun!," he said. "Because they go out and take no prisoners. Don't apologize for anything. Get one hundred people and take the street."[37] The protests also introduced many USC students to union organizing. In May 1998 Lawson held an alternative, social justice graduation for striking workers and students. "We had a street drama on commencement day where we took over the intersection at Exposition and Figueroa," Lawson remembered. "While the commencement was going on inside with Bill Cosby as the speaker, we were on the outside doing a commencement for the people who got degrees in justice." Thirty-nine demonstrators wore caps and gowns and received a "diploma for justice" before being arrested for blocking the intersection.[38]

The protests shamed USC for creating poverty in surrounding low-income neighborhoods and exposed the administration's attempt to wall off the campus from what it called "environmental threats"—crime in the surrounding neighborhood.[39] Durazo pointed out that the issue of fair employment had a direct impact on the broader community.

> These in fact are workers who live in the immediate community. They work at USC, they live in the immediate neighborhoods of USC, they go to church in the churches surrounding USC, and their children go to the schools surrounding USC. There is a strong, now joint community and worker effort to ensure that USC treats the community with greater respect.[40]

Local 11 and USC reached a settlement in October 1999. Under the new five-year contract, the USC food service and janitorial staff retained their jobs and their benefits.

Dolores Huerta, Rabbi Steven Jacobs, Rev. James M. Lawson Jr., and Rev. Jesse Jackson (left to right) celebrate the signing of HERE Local 11's contract with the University of Southern California on October 5, 1999. *Courtesy of James M. Lawson Jr.*

THE LIVING WAGE CAMPAIGN

Local 11's success in creating broad labor and community alliances and engaging political leaders provided the foundation for the 1997 passage of a living wage ordinance in Los Angeles. In the living wage campaign, hotel workers linked their experiences to the conditions of poverty faced by the working class as a whole. As the union's first legislative victory, the ordinance revealed the power of the renascent labor movement to reshape city politics, and it propelled a national movement for a living wage.

The immediate impetus for the living wage campaign was a policy change at the Los Angeles International Airport in 1995 that broke up union jobs and distributed them into a mix of private- and public-sector contracts. Two private contracts were awarded to the McDonalds fast-food chain, which immediately proceeded to fire the union employees and offer to rehire them in positions offering only the minimum wage and no benefits. The outsourcing was part of Mayor Richard Riordan's push to privatize city services to cut municipal costs. At the airport, this push for privatization threatened one thousand unionized workers, mostly African Americans and Latinos. Local 11 estimated that the contract changes could result in the loss of over fifteen million dollars for the communities in which airport workers lived. Local 11 decided to mount a campaign aimed at passing a city council ordinance that would guarantee that any job within the city's jurisdiction would pay a living wage.

Local 11's success at building alliances resulted in the formation of the powerful Los Angeles Living Wage Coalition. The living wage campaign was coordinated by the Los Angeles Alliance for a New Economy (LAANE), an organization that Durazo helped create in 1993.[41] Led by attorney Madeline Janis-Aparicio, LAANE published economic policy analyses that made the case for a living wage by revealing the extent of working poverty at local and national levels. Lawson's outreach with clergy led to the foundation of Clergy and Laity United for Economic Justice (CLUE-LA) in 1996. Drawing on his experience as chair of the Memphis sanitation strike in 1968, Lawson persuaded his colleagues to join the fight for a living wage. "We religious figures had a responsibility because we needed to know what people in congregations were doing for income," he said. "We had to be aware of the underemployment and unemployment problem with our

Rev. Lawson spoke about **what it was like in the civil rights movement** and César spoke about what it was like to create a **union for farmworkers** when everybody said it can't be done and when you were faced with violence and faced with attacks. So can you imagine what a historic moment to have those two leaders speak to hotel workers? **And it made all the difference in the world**. We got our second wind, went back, figured out how to restrategize, what kinds of new tactics to use, and we eventually won.
—Maria Elena Durazo April 2013

congregations. We had to be aware of what we ourselves were paying our support people, our janitors."[42] CLUE-LA mobilized congregations, lobbied city councilmembers, and participated in nonviolent actions.

To make the case for a living wage, the Los Angeles Living Wage Coalition highlighted the inadequacy of the minimum wage and the moral responsibility of the city to pay fair wages. Organizers argued that people working full time—who often had to hold multiple jobs to make ends meet—should be able live above the poverty line and provide for their families. "These were jobs that the city was responsible for," Durazo explained. "Anything that belongs to the city and people work there, [that company] ought to pay a living wage. Any contract the city issues, the workers for that company have to make a living wage."[43] Organizers bolstered this argument with testimony from workers, as campaign media director Bobbi Murray noted.

> Workers came to city hall and testified about injuries that went untreated because there was no time off permitted for a doctor visit and no insurance or way to pay for it anyway. Families crowded into tiny one-bedroom apartments in dangerous areas of town just to make rent and visits to food pantries to manage the groceries every month.[44]

CLUE-LA's acts of civil disobedience and its direct lobbying attracted a wide range of community allies to the living wage campaign.[45] City councilmembers who might have otherwise opposed the living wage ordinance voted for it because of the pressure of influential religious leaders in their district. "We had clergy visitations to every council person, and if it didn't take the first time, there were continued visitations to help them decide that this was something the city could do," Lawson recalled.[46] Jackie Goldberg, a councilwoman who became a key advocate for the ordinance, agreed. "I think [CLUE-LA] had a significant effect on public opinion, which overwhelmingly supported the living wage in spite of the mayor's sentiment," she told the *Los Angeles Times*. "A lot of the popularity came because the coalition was reaching out to people in communities, in churches and synagogues."[47]

Durazo and Lawson convened a meeting at Holman United Methodist Church with clergy from a number of denominations to discuss the ramifications of the policy shift. Durazo recalled that these leaders were concerned for their congregants.

> Clergy after clergy leader said, "We are already having more people in our food lines." So this connection was made between these workers and the churches who were saying, "We're now starting to get more and more families, more and more people, who can't survive on what they're getting paid." So it was putting pressure on the churches to figure out how do you come up with more food and resources for this community.[48]

Lawson saw his participation in the living wage campaign as an integral part of his ministry.

> How do you sit down to counsel and pray with a member that's been downsized without recognizing the role of downsizing, the corporate mind that developed a value system that excluded the employee as a value or asset? How do you compartmentalize your pastoral care?[49]

On November 22, 1996, the Los Angeles Living Wage Coalition won an important preliminary victory by pushing through the city council a worker retention ordinance for workers at Los Angeles International Airport. Directly responding to the type of outsourcing that occurred at the airport, the city council declared that the city would retain any worker that was laid off as a result of the replacement of one city contractor with another.[50]

Rev. James M. Lawson Jr. participates in a march in Los Angeles. *Courtesy of Rev. James M. Lawson Jr.*

On March 18, 1997, the hard work of the coalition of labor unions, religious groups, and community organizations paid off. The city council passed the measure unanimously and later overrode the veto of Mayor Riordan.

The Los Angeles living wage ordinance set an important precedent for workers' rights and provided a new organizing platform for community-labor movements.[51] The law was the first in the nation to include provisions for health benefits and to prohibit retaliation by employers against their workers. The living wage law applied to all city-leased properties, city-employed contractors, contractors requiring city operating permits, and recipients of city financial assistance.[52] The city wage level is adjusted annually to ensure that workers can support themselves and their families in future economic conditions. Kent Wong, director of the UCLA Labor Center, noted that "the living wage movement spread nationally, so what happened in Los Angeles helped pace the nation for a broader agenda for economic justice." Within a decade, over 120 living wage ordinances had been passed across the country.[53]

The passage of the living wage ordinance demonstrated the political power that Local 11 had built. In subsequent years the union increasingly focused on electoral organizing. As head of the Los Angeles Federation of Labor, Contreras mobilized powerful grassroots political actions. Instead of having unions endorse and contribute to political candidates, union workers hit the streets to register voters and raise awareness of the political issues that affected them. Labor become a powerful force in the immigrant rights movement, which continued to draw inspiration from the civil rights and farmworkers' movements.

In 2003 Durazo became the national director of the Immigrant Workers' Freedom Ride, a bus ride from Los Angeles to Washington, DC, that was modeled on the Freedom Rides in the 1960s. The Immigrant Workers' Freedom Ride helped build a national movement to embrace the humanity of immigrant workers in the United States. Durazo also shaped national labor politics as the chair of the AFL-CIO's Immigration Committee. In 2006 she succeeded her late husband as the head of the Los Angeles County Federation of Labor, where she continued to advance a culture of nonviolence and social justice in the labor movement. She left the position in 2014 to become UNITE HERE's general vice president for immigration, civil rights, and diversity.

The philosophy and strategy of nonviolence enabled Local 11 to revive social justice unionism. Learning nonviolent tactics and applying them in creative ways transformed the union and its members. Workers became leaders who extended their fight beyond the workplace into neighborhoods and built labor and community alliances across the lines of race, ethnicity, and citizenship. Durazo noted that the impact of Local 11 extended far beyond the city of Los Angeles.

> What we established in Local 11 in terms of creating this culture, not only around nonviolence, but around other ways of organizing, connecting to the community, home visits, and different ways of being more effective in our goals, spread and was adopted across the national union. Many of the organizers from Local 11 went to work [for] or were asked to help other locals in other parts of the country and other cities. Eventually, the rank and file were promoted to be full-time organizers, [and] full-time organizers became leads and then directors. A lot of this has been planting the seed in other places. Today there are very few places I could go to in HERE where some if not all of the elements are being used naturally there.[54]

NOTES

This chapter draws extensively from interviews of Rev. Lawson and guest speakers that were held during a special topics course sponsored by the Labor Center, the César E. Chávez Department of Chicana/o Studies, the Labor and Workplace Studies Minor, the Department of African American Studies, and the History Department at UCLA.

1. James M. Lawson Jr. and Maria Elena Durazo, discussion with Kent Wong and Kelly Lytle Hernandez, May 29, 2013, Los Angeles.

2. Ibid.

3. Ibid.

4. Interview segment in *The New Los Angeles*, DVD, directed by Lyn Goldfarb (Berkeley, CA: Berkeley Media, 2005).

5. Lawson and Durazo, discussion with Wong and Lytle Hernandez, May 29, 2013.

6. Ibid.

7. Ibid.

8. "Latina Will Head Hotel Workers Union," *Los Angeles Times*, April 21, 1989, http://articles.latimes.com/1989-04-21/local/me-2227_1_hotel-and-restaurant-workers-maria-elena-durazo-restaurant-employees-union; and Bob Sipchen, "Labor of Love," *Los Angeles Times*, March 9, 1997, http://articles.latimes.com/1997-03-09/news/ls-36265_1_labor-movement.

9. Quoted in Marita Hernandez, "Organizer Wins Post of President: Latina Leads Takeover of Union from Anglo Males," *Los Angeles Times*, May 6, 1989, http://articles.latimes.com/1989-05-06/news/mn-2087_1_durazo-s-english-union-from-anglo-males-maria-elena-durazo.

10. Bob Baker, "Union, Hyatt Hotels Still at Odds," *Los Angeles Times*, July 23, 1991, http://articles.latimes.com/1991-07-23/local/me-294_1_employee-work-schedules.

11. Bob Baker, "Arrests Fan Hotel's Labor Dispute," *Los Angeles Times*, October 18, 1989, http://articles.latimes.com/1989-10-18/local/me-362_1_hotel-workers.

12. Nancy Rivera Brooks, "Hyatt Touch Leaves Labor Touchy," *Los Angeles Times*, September 27, 1990, http://articles.latimes.com/1990-09-27/business/fi-1844_1_hyatt-hotels.

13. Lawson and Durazo, discussion with Wong and Lytle Hernandez.

14. Ibid.

15. Ibid.

16. Ibid.

17. Rivera Brooks, "Hyatt Touch Leaves Labor Touchy."

18. Rodolfo Acuña, *Anything But Mexican: Chicanos in Contemporary Los Angeles* (New York: Verso, 1996), 182.

19. Kim Geron, "Hotel Workers Defeat the Hyatt Touch," *Labor Note*s (Detroit), December 1991.

20. Lawson and Durazo, discussion with Wong and Lytle Hernandez.

21. Ibid.

22. Ibid.

23. Quoted in Patricia Konley, compiler, "Platform: 'Leaders Must Be Willing to Take Risks, Sacrifice,'" *Los Angeles Times*, November 22, 1993, http://articles.latimes.com/1993-11-22/local/me-59560_1_leader.

24. Lawson's four steps for a nonviolent campaign are discussed in chapter 1.

25. Maria Elena Durazo, "Maria Elena Durazo: Controversial Local Union Head Takes No Prisoners to Win the Point," interview by Steve Proffitt, *Los Angeles Times*, September 27, 1992, http://articles.latimes.com/1992-09-27/opinion/op-486_1_los-angeles.

26. Patrick J. McDonnell, "37 Protesters Arrested in Hotel Labor Dispute," *Los Angeles Times*, December 2, 1994, http://articles.latimes.com/1994-12-02/local/me-4183_1_union-contract.

27. Karen Brodkin, "The Context of Labor and Immigrant Workers: Rights Activism in Los Angeles," in *Making Democracy Matter: Identity and Activism in Los Angeles* (New Brunswick, NJ: Rutgers University Press, 2007), 17–42.

28. Bob Baker, "Korean Firm Fires Staff in Hyatt Wilshire Takeover," *Los Angeles Times*, January 1, 1992, http://articles.latimes.com/1992-01-01/local/me-1092_1_hyatt-workers.

29. Timothy Williams, "Sit-in at S. Korean Consulate Protests Hotel's Labor Policies," *Los Angeles Times*, September 25, 1992, http://articles.latimes.com/1992-09-25/local/me-902_1_south-korean-consulate; Eric Malnic, "Hotel Accepts Union, Will Rehire Workers," *Los Angeles Times*, October 23, 1992, http://articles.latimes.com/1992-10-23/local/me-676_1_wilshire-plaza-hotel; and Jake Doherty, "Hotel Labor Pact: Room for Everyone," *Los Angeles Times*, November 1, 1992, http://articles.latimes.com/1992-11-01/news/ci-1937_1_wilshire-plaza-hotel. The organization changed its name in 2006 to Koreatown Immigrant Workers Alliance.

30. K. Connie Kang, "UCLA Class Puts Theory to Test in the Real World," *Los Angeles Times*, March 11,1995, http://articles.latimes.com/1995-03-11/local/me-41292_1_asian-american-studies.

31. UNITED HERE Local 11, *City on the Edge*, YouTube video, 12:36, posted by uniteherevideos, September 21, 2010, http://www.youtube.com/watch?v=i6gDA0Agh3M.

32. Robert D. Wilton and Cynthia Cranford, "Toward an Understanding of the Spatiality of Social Movements," *Social Problems* 49, no. 3 (2002): 374–94.

33. Lawson and Durazo, discussion with Wong and Lytle Hernandez.

34. Maria Elena Durazo, "Fasting to Right Worker Injustices," *Los Angeles Times*, May 25, 1999, http://articles.latimes.com/1999/may/25/local/me-40625; and Donna Houston and Laura Pulido, "The Work of Performativity: Staging Social Justice at the University of California," in *Critical Theories, Radical Pedagogies, and Global Conflicts,* ed. Gustavo Fishman (Oxford: Rowman and Littlefield Publishers, 2005), 317–42.

35. Quoted in Peter Y. Hong, "Fasting Union Leader Asks City Council to Influence USC," *Los Angeles Times*, May 19, 1999.

36. Durazo, "Fasting to Right Worker Injustices."

37. Quoted in Laura Pulido, "The Roots of Political Consciousness among Militant Unionists and Worker Activists in Los Angeles" (paper, Southern California Studies Center, University of Southern California, 2008), http://www.usc.edu/dept/LAS/SC2/pdf/pulido.pdf.

38. Lawson and Durazo, discussion with Wong and Lytle Hernandez.

39. Ted Rorlich, "USC Workers Launch Fast in Job Dispute," *Los Angeles Times*, November 19, 1998.

40. "California University Workers Hold Hunger Strike," *Democracy Now!* (radio and television news program), November 16, 1998, http://www.democracynow.org/1998/11/16/california_university_workers_hold_hunger_strike.

41. Reflecting its roots in Local 11 organizing, LAANE was originally called the Tourism Industry Development Council (TIDC).

42. Lawson and Durazo, discussion with Wong and Lytle Hernandez.

43. Ibid.

44. Bobbi Murray, "Organize! Living Wage Lives in LA," *Shelterforce*, January/February 1998, http://www.nhi.org/online/issues/97/organize.html.

45. Forrest Stuart, "From the Shop to the Streets: UNITE HERE Organizing in Los Angeles Hotels," in *Working for Justice: The L.A. Model of Organizing and Advocacy*, ed. Ruth Milkman, Joshua Bloom, and Victor Narro (Cornell University Press, 2010), 194–210.

46. Quoted in Danny Feingold, "Putting Faith in Labor," *Los Angeles Times*, August 28, 1998, http://articles.latimes.com/1998/aug/28/news/ls-17211/3; and Lawson and Durazo, discussion with Wong and Lytle Hernandez.

47. Quoted in Feingold, "Putting Faith in Labor."

48. Lawson and Durazo, discussion with Wong and Lytle Hernandez.

49. Quoted in David Reynolds, "The Living Wage Movement Sweeps the Nation," *WorkingUSA* 3, no. 3 (1999): 61.

50. Madeline Janis-Arparicio, Steve Cancian, and Gary Phillips, "Building a Movement for a Living Wage," *Poverty and Race* 5, no. 1 (1996): 33–63.

51. Bobbi Murray, "Living Wage Come of Age: An Increasingly Sophisticated Movement Has Put Opponents on the Defensive," *The Nation*, July 23, 2001.

52. Larry Frank and Kent Wong, "Dynamic Political Mobilization: The Los Angeles County Federation of Labor," *WorkingUSA* 8, no. 2 (2004): 155–81.

53. Bobbi Murray, *Arcing toward Justice: The Evolution of the Living Wage Movement* (San Francisco: Tides Foundation, 2002), http://www.tides.org/fileadmin/user/pdf/TidesFoundation_ArcingTowardJustice.pdf.

54. Lawson and Durazo, discussion with Wong and Lytle Hernandez.

Rev. James M. Lawson Jr. speaks to undocumented students at the launch of the first Dream Summer at the University of California, Los Angeles, June 16, 2011. *Courtesy of Pocho Sanchez.*

CHAPTER 6

UNDOCUMENTED AND UNAFRAID: THE IMMIGRANT YOUTH MOVEMENT

Alma Mirell Castrejon

In the sight of GOD there is no illegal human being.
In the sight of creation there is no undocumented person.
— James M. Lawson Jr., lecture given
at the University of California, Los Angeles, 2015

On the morning of June 15, 2012, over two hundred undocumented immigrant youth converged in front of the US federal building in downtown Los Angeles. News had spread that President Barack Obama would make an important announcement on a new immigration policy that afternoon. Demonstrators stopped traffic in front of the federal building, held a sit-in on a nearby freeway on-ramp, and blocked the bus entrance to the Metropolitan Detention Center, where hundreds of undocumented immigrants are held every day, waiting to be deported.[1] The slogan passionately chanted by these young people—"Undocumented and Unafraid!"—has come to symbolize the power of undocumented immigrant youth who have emerged from the shadows.

A few hours later, the majority of the demonstrators gathered at the UCLA Downtown Labor Center to watch live coverage of the announcement from the White House. The president announced a new policy, Deferred Action for Childhood Arrivals (DACA), that would stop the deportation of undocumented immigrant youth. An estimated 1.4 million undocumented immigrant youth would quality for the program, giving them a two-year reprieve from deportation and a work permit, and in some cases it would offer them the opportunity to apply for "advance parole" to travel outside the country.[2] The emotion and the energy in the room as Obama made the announcement were overwhelming. Many of the undocumented youth activists watching the press conference had played key roles in the campaign that had preceded the administration's decision. Many cried, held hands, or embraced while paying close attention to each word the president said.

DACA, the first federal policy since the 1986 Immigration Reform and Control Act (IRCA) to touch a large number of immigrants, will improve the lives of hundreds of thousands of people.[3] Although it is a limited and temporary solution to the broken immigration system in the United States, it was a historic victory that exemplifies the courage, spirit, tenacity, and energy of the immigrant youth movement. Inspired by the rich history of other social movements and grounded in the power of nonviolence, the immigrant youth movement has been driven by a commitment to dignity, equality, and social justice.

A DECADE IN THE SHADOWS

Undocumented youth in the United States have struggled for years to obtain the right to pursue a postsecondary education. In 1982, in *Plyler v. Doe*, the US Supreme Court affirmed the constitutional right to a free public education for undocumented children in kindergarten through twelfth grade. The case concerned a section of the Texas Education Code that attempted to bar undocumented students from public schools by requiring schools to ask for proof of citizenship and to deny admission to students who could not provide proper documentation. The Court ruled that all children, regardless of immigration status, were entitled to a public education, but the decision did not address access to higher education.[4] In 1996 the US Congress passed the Illegal Immigration Reform and Immigrant Responsibility Act (IIRIRA), which sought to streamline US immigration laws and increase their enforcement. Section 505 prohibits states from granting higher education benefits to undocumented students if those same benefits are not available to US citizens as well.[5] These two legal documents—the Court's decision in *Plyler* and the IIRIRA—defined access to post-secondary education for undocumented immigrant youth at the end of the twentieth century.

In 2001 the vast majority of undocumented youth were living in the shadows. Almost no one would publicly disclose undocumented immigration status. The Development Relief and Education for Alien Minors (DREAM) Act, introduced in Congress in August of that year, offered hope to the undocumented immigrant students who wanted to earn a college degree. Attached to a comprehensive immigration reform bill, the DREAM Act was intended to increase access to higher education and to provide a pathway to citizenship for these youth. The DREAM Act would grant a six-year conditional residency period for young people who qualified. Undocumented immigrant youth who had entered the United States before the age of sixteen, had graduated from a US high school or obtained a GED, and demonstrated good moral character would be eligible to adjust their immigration status.[6] Upon completion of the six-year conditional period, those who completed either college or 910 hours of community service would qualify for legal permanent resident (LPR) status and could then apply for citizenship. The DREAM Act failed to garner enough support to come to the floor for a vote.

In 2001 there were no state or national networks advocating for federal legislation that would protect the rights of immigrant youth, but undocumented youth were beginning to receive some support at the state level. A number of states enacted legislation that grants undocumented students access to public colleges and universities by allowing them to pay in-state tuition rates. Texas was the first to pass such legislation in 2001, followed by California, Utah, New York, Washington, Illinois, Kansas, New Mexico, Nebraska, Maryland, Connecticut, Colorado, Minnesota, New Jersey, Oregon, and Florida.[7] In Oklahoma and Rhode Island, in-state tuition rates for undocumented students were approved by the states' boards of regents, and the University of Hawaii and the University of Michigan adopted in-state tuition policies through decisions by boards of regents. In Virginia, students who qualify under DACA can pay in-state tuition rates.[8] To qualify for in-state tuition, students are typically required to meet the state's residency requirements, to have attended high school and received either a high school diploma or a GED, to be enrolled in a two- or four-year college or university, and to file an affidavit stating their intention to

> For DREAM Act students, **going to college** is itself an **act of civil disobedience**.
> —Rev. Lawson June 2011

apply for legal residency as soon as the opportunity is available. Five states restricted access to higher education for undocumented students. Arizona, Indiana, and Georgia prohibit undocumented students from receiving in-state tuition rates, and South Carolina and Alabama prohibit undocumented students from enrolling in public colleges.[9]

Momentum began to build in 2004 as student support and community advocacy groups began emerging, especially on college and university campuses in states with tuition equity bills. The Student Immigrant Movement (SIM) in Massachusetts and the University Leadership Initiative (ULI) in Texas, both founded in 2005, were among the first student organizations established. In California, various campus support groups were created to help students with the difficulties of navigating college as an undocumented student. The California Dream Network (CDN), a statewide association of campus immigrant student organizations, formed in 2006 and held its first retreat in December to solidify the network and to begin addressing the issues impacting California's undocumented students. This newly formed network supported undocumented students throughout their educational journey, and members began working on local and state issues such as access to financial aid and driver licenses and developing campus-specific initiatives to support undocumented students. The dissemination of information through policy briefs, workshop presentations, and sharing stories created a foundation for future advocacy.

In California undocumented students who had graduated from college began forming community groups that focused on immigrant rights more broadly. These young leaders saw the need to promote activism in the surrounding community, not just on campus. Orange County Immigrant Youth United (OCIYU), formerly known as the Orange County Dream Team (OCDT), was formed in 2004, and Dream Team Los Angeles (DTLA) was formed in 2009 by many of the same people who had founded support groups on college campuses years before. These activities were mirrored in other states.

Undocumented youth had begun to connect with other activists across the country through social media by 2007. Later that year seven undocumented students joined a chat room in a DREAM Act forum and started the action-oriented website DreamActivist.org, which would become the online hub for the DREAM Act campaign and the immigrant youth movement. By 2008 an informal national coalition of undocumented youth leaders had launched United We Dream (UWD). In December of that year, with the support of the National Immigration Law Center (NILC), undocumented leaders, advocates, and allies from various parts of the United States convened in Washington, DC. Two goals emerged from this meeting: to build UWD into a national organization, and to take the lead on the campaign to pass the DREAM Act. The legislation had again failed to pass

Congress in 2007, even though the community service requirement had been replaced with service in the United States military to make the legislation more appealing to conservative members of Congress. These decisions set the tone for the future of the undocumented immigrant youth movement. Undocumented youth were no longer following the direction of major immigrant rights organizations and advocates; instead, they were at the forefront of efforts to persuade Congress to pass the legislation.

The 2008 presidential election provided opportunities for immigrant youth to campaign for a candidate who promised to support the immigrant community. The Obama for America (OFA) campaign embraced a national grassroots organizing approach. Undocumented youth found inspiration from a presidential candidate who promised to pass the DREAM Act and advocated comprehensive immigration reform. In the months leading to the presidential election, many undocumented youth throughout the country joined efforts to elect Obama by canvassing in their communities, making phone calls, and traveling to swing states to help with the campaign. Obama ran on the promise of hope and change, words that resonated deeply with undocumented youth.

COMING OUT OF THE SHADOWS

Undocumented youth gained a new sense of hope when the DREAM Act was reintroduced in March 2009, and by late 2009 they were shifting the national discourse on immigration through their public efforts. Although many undocumented youth organizers believed that the DREAM Act had a better chance of passing Congress than comprehensive immigration reform, the leadership of the Democratic Party and mainstream immigrant rights organizations advocated exclusively for a comprehensive bill.[10] They embraced an all-or-nothing strategy, fearing that a piecemeal approach would never attain the larger immigration reform needed, even though similar strategies had failed numerous times over the years.

One of the first actions that captured the attention of the country was the Trail of Dreams. A fifteen-hundred-mile pilgrimage on foot from Florida to Washington, DC, it recalled the marches made in support of other social justice movements, including the farmworkers' march led by César Chávez in 1996. On January 1, 2010, Felipe Matos, Carlos Roa, Juan Rodriguez, and Gaby Pacheco began the journey to the nation's capital. They met with hundreds of people, shared their stories as undocumented youth, and changed the hearts and minds of many through their conversations. The four youth encountered hatred and endured racial slurs during this bold undertaking and were even threatened by the Ku Klux Klan, but they remained strong and adhered to the principles of nonviolence.[11] Their courage captured the attention of immigrant youth across the nation, who followed the Trail of Dreams through mainstream and social media. The four arrived in Washington, DC, on May 1, after a four-month journey.

On March 10, 2010, the first National Coming Out day of action took place. In Chicago, Los Angeles, New York, Washington, DC, Miami, Phoenix, and other cities across the nation, hundreds of undocumented youth held public actions to declare that they were undocumented and unafraid. The term *coming out* was inspired by the lesbian, gay, bisexual, transgender, and queer (LGBTQ) movement, which had shown that only by coming out publicly could LGBTQ people realize their rights. Many of the first students to join the DREAM Act campaign identified as queer as well as undocumented. National Coming Out marked a turning point for the immigrant youth movement. From this point on, many undocumented youth used their own names instead of pseudonyms and appeared publicly in the media instead of using blurred or darkened images when speaking about their status.

Through the use of traditional and social media, organizers reached out to thousands of immigrant youth and conveyed the message that undocumented status should be

Trail of Dreams activists in Apopka, Florida, on January 21, 2010. *Courtesy of Adrian Sanchez.*

a source of empowerment and a call to action rather than a source of shame and fear. In the following months, undocumented youth intensified their campaigns to pressure elected officials to support the DREAM Act. The National Coming Out actions were crucial for mobilizing youth across the country, and by May a group of undocumented youth had formed The Dream Is Coming, a project whose goal was to plan a series of actions to escalate the DREAM Act campaign.

As undocumented youth were increasing their visibility and gaining support for the DREAM Act, states like Arizona were pushing for anti-immigrant legislation. On April 23, 2010, Arizona signed into law a draconian anti-immigrant bill, Senate Bill 1070, which criminalized undocumented immigrants and encouraged racial profiling. Many undocumented youth leaders joined efforts to challenge SB 1070 and publicly stood in solidarity with the Arizona immigrant community.

Tragedy struck on May 15 as two leaders of the immigrant youth movement, Tam Tran and Cinthya Felix, were killed in a car accident. Tran and Felix had been leaders of IDEAS (Improving Dreams, Education, Access and Success), an undocumented student organization at UCLA. Both were UCLA alumni who went on to enroll in graduate school (Tran at Brown and Felix at Columbia), and they were among the first immigrant students to go public with their stories. Tran had testified in Congress to advocate passage of the DREAM Act in 2007 and had appeared in the national media. A memorial held at UCLA on May 17 was attended by more than five hundred people, including a broad network of undocumented immigrant youth activists who had worked with IDEAS since its formation.

Also on May 17, four undocumented youth and one ally—Lizbeth Mateo, Mohammad Abdollahi, Tania Unzueta, Yahaira Carrillo, and Raúl Alcaraz—held a sit-in inside Senator John McCain's office in Tucson, Arizona, to demand his support for the DREAM Act. McCain had previously been a co-sponsor of the bill, but pressure from anti-immigrant groups had persuaded him to retract his support. The youth, known as the Dream Act 5, had planned the action for May 17 because it marked the fifty-sixth anniversary of the US Supreme Court's decision in *Brown v. Board of Education*, which called for the elimination of racially segregated public schools. Each of the five wore a button with a photo of Tran and Felix to honor their memory. The sit-in was the first act of civil disobedience ever led by undocumented youth, and it sent shock waves through the immigrant rights community. Many were stunned by the bold action, and some opposed the risky approach.

Such disagreements have historical parallels. The nonviolent direct action campaigns of the Student Nonviolent Coordinating Committee (SNCC) in the 1960s were met with disapproval and opposition from older and more cautious civil rights organizations like the National Association for the Advancement of Colored People (NAACP).[12] Similarly, the Arizona sit-in was not condoned by some of the mainstream immigrant rights organizations that, along with the Congressional Hispanic Caucus, continued to oppose the DREAM Act as a stand-alone bill. Despite the controversy, the action galvanized and strengthened the immigrant youth movement. By engaging in civil disobedience and risking arrest and deportation—at that time an unfathomable tactic—the Dream Act 5 made history. They inspired thousands to lose their fear, to come out of the shadows, and to join the movement to advance a national campaign for the DREAM Act as a stand-alone bill.

In the months that followed, undocumented youth organized hundreds of nonviolent actions throughout the country, including press conferences, phone banks, vigils, town hall meetings, marches, rallies, hunger strikes, and other forms of civil disobedience. These actions gained unprecedented support for the DREAM Act. Hundreds of thousands of calls were made to Congress as a result of the massive organizing effort, which was generated exclusively by volunteers.

To further advance the demand for the DREAM Act as a stand-alone bill, nine young people—the Wilshire 9—held a sit-in on Wilshire Boulevard on May 20 in front of the West Los Angeles Federal Building, blocking traffic on one of the busiest thoroughfares in Los Angeles. Coincidentally, one of the hosts of the *John and Ken Show,* a right-wing talk radio show, was caught in the massive traffic jam. Angered by the demonstration, he and his co-host launched an on-the-air hate campaign against Nancy Meza, a UCLA student activist who served as the media coordinator for the Wilshire 9 action. They encouraged listeners to demand that Meza be deported, broadcast her email address and mobile number, and even promoted the sale of T-shirts printed with the telephone number of US Immigration and Customs Enforcement (ICE) and the slogan "Deport Nancy Meza." Throughout the weeks that followed, Meza received hundreds of racist and violent threats. In spite of the hate campaign, Meza graduated from UCLA and began working full time as an immigrant youth activist.

Just two weeks after the Wilshire 9 action, twelve undocumented youth and their allies began the Dream Freedom Ride, a caravan from Los Angeles to Washington inspired by the Freedom Rides that challenged Jim Crow. Along the way, the group met with labor, faith-based, and immigrant rights groups, organized press and educational events, and lobbied elected officials in key states. The nonviolence teachings of Rev. James M. Lawson Jr. were integrated into the planning meetings and training sessions for Dream Freedom Ride. This training became especially important as immigrant youth crossed the state line from California into Arizona, where they risked arrest and deportation. Once the twelve riders arrived in Washington, DC, they began working with other undocumented youth who had gathered in the capital to launch Dream University, a series of public seminars and "teach-ins" on immigration.

Another group of immigrant youth activists held a nonviolent demonstration in the halls of Congress. On July 20, twenty-one undocumented youth from Arizona, California, Illinois, Kansas, Michigan, Missouri, New York, and Virginia entered the Senate building and began sit-ins in a number of offices. These undocumented youth had prepared for months for this action, which was the first act of civil disobedience by undocumented youth in a federal building. They risked detention in federal facilities and deportation and separation from their families and friends. All were arrested, but they were not placed in deportation hearings.

While the sit-ins were taking place in Washington, DC, undocumented undergraduate and graduate students in Southern California commenced a hunger strike outside the LA office of Senator Dianne Feinstein. Organizers from Dream Team Los Angeles, Orange Country Dream Team, and San Fernando Valley Dream Team organized the action in solidarity with the twenty-one who were arrested in Washington, DC. Their purpose was to step up the pressure on Feinstein to champion the DREAM Act as a separate bill. UCLA student activist Carlos Amador and queer undocumented activist Jorge Gutierrez were two of the youth who participated in the fifteen-day hunger strike. During those two weeks they met with Feinstein's staff and gathered the support of hundreds of individuals, organizations, and undocumented youth throughout Southern California. Amador reflected on the importance of the action.

> One of the outcomes of the hunger strike was to bring a sense of urgency to our Southern California community. In a period of fifteen days, we had over three hundred people visit us from different states. For the first time we had Methodist pastors and the Jewish community who came to visit us, and groups of children from after-school programs. Our parents would ride the bus for an hour to come visit us. Passersby would ask us about the action, and we got a chance to explain our stories. They themselves would make calls to senators right there. We generated a lot of buzz around the issue. Camping outside the senator's office made us visible. Even though Senator Feinstein did not move on the bill, we were able to mobilize many people. The hunger strike helped us galvanize a lot of the work in Southern California and helped us push the issue of immigration and the DREAM Act campaign to the finish line in the following months.[13]

Undocumented students stage a sit-in in John McCain's senatorial office in Tucson, May 7, 2010. *Courtesy of Adrian Sanchez.*

We are a **mirror of the gift of life** in that we can make **the choice to give ourselves to a cause** and to a way of life that is much larger than we are. We can give ourselves **to a work that we will never succeed** in fulfilling.

—Rev. Lawson April 2013

Similar actions were held throughout the country by undocumented youth who were demanding the passage of the DREAM Act as a stand-alone bill. In North Carolina, Viridiana Martínez, Loida Silva, and Rosario López fasted for thirteen days to demand Senator Kay Hagan's support for the bill. The longest hunger strike was held in Texas, where the group DREAM Act NOW held a rolling hunger strike for forty-five days. Hunger strikes were also held in Arizona, Indiana, and Minnesota.

On September 21, 2010, the DREAM Act was brought to a vote. It had been incorporated into the National Defense Authorization Act for 2011, together with a provision that would repeal the Don't Ask Don't Tell (DADT) policy, which protected closeted LGBTQ persons serving in the US military from discrimination and harassment while barring from service those who were openly nonheterosexual. The bill's supporters could not gather the sixty votes needed to avoid a filibuster in the Senate.[14] Youth activists began planning acts of civil disobedience to demand reintroduction of the bill. Sit-ins were conducted in senators' offices in Washington, DC, and Utah, and hunger strikes took place in Indiana, Texas, and Arizona. On December 8 the DREAM Act passed the House of Representatives by a vote of 216 to 198, a huge breakthrough for the immigrant youth movement.[15]

Undocumented youth across the country were ecstatic and hopeful that the DREAM Act would also pass in the Senate. The legislation reached the Senate floor on December 18, 2010. Throughout the country, undocumented youth gathered to watch the live broadcast of the vote. At the UCLA Labor Center, dozens of youth, parents, allies, and supporters gathered, tense and anxious. As soon as the DREAM Act came up for a vote, everyone fell silent. One by one the "Yeas" and the "Nays" were announced. The bill needed sixty votes to avoid a filibuster, but only obtained fifty-five. The DREAM Act had failed by five votes. Some stood in silent disbelief, while some began to cry. Others were in denial and hoped that there would be a recount. When the reality set in, some dropped to their knees, crying and screaming. Moments later people began speaking out, sharing their feelings with those around them. Although people expressed pain and anger, their determination was unshaken.

Neidi Dominguez, an organizer with DREAM Team Los Angeles, consulted with the statewide organizer of the California Dream Network (CDN), which, along with the Coalition for Humane Immigrant Rights of Los Angeles (CHIRLA), was hosting a viewing event less than a mile away. The two activists decided that both groups would join together in solidarity for a march in MacArthur Park. Dominguez recalled how their anger and the frustration turned into action.

> I got to see the vote take place. I was there at the Labor Center with dozens of other Dreamers. We first felt hopeful. When we were five votes short, it was heartbreaking. There were lots of tears, and it was very emotional. I was sad, but I was more upset to see that five absentee votes by Democrats kept us stuck in limbo. Despite putting ourselves out there, risking safety to ourselves and our families, going through sit-ins and risking deportation. Afterward, I felt angry. I realized this was not the end. Immediately, we took to the streets in MacArthur Park.[16]

This defeat of the DREAM Act transformed the campaign into a national movement. Within a few months greater numbers of undocumented youth came out of the shadows, determined to build alliances and to challenge the unjust immigration policies that criminalize and oppress the immigrant community.

LESSONS FROM THE CIVIL RIGHTS MOVEMENT

Many of the actions of civil disobedience that were staged to support passage of the DREAM Act were directly influenced by the civil rights movement, the farmworkers' movement, and the LGBTQ movement. Youth activists borrowed strategies, tactics, concepts, and slogans to advance their campaigns. Many immigrant youth leaders had been exposed to the philosophy of nonviolence, and they generated discussion on nonviolence as part of the organizing process. The fasts led by César Chávez in Delano, California, inspired the immigrant youth to launch hunger strikes in California and Texas. The lunch counter sit-ins in Nashville inspired sit-ins in the streets, in government offices, and in the halls of Congress. The Dream Freedom caravan from Los Angeles to Washington, DC, was inspired by the Freedom Rides more than fifty years earlier.

One notable campaign in 2009 brought together immigrant youth and veterans of the civil rights movement. Members of the Student Immigrant Movement (SIM) made a pilgrimage from Boston to the South to meet members of the Clinton 12 and the Little Rock 9, who were among the first students to desegregate public schools in Tennessee and Arkansas in the 1950s.[17] SIM members traveled to Clinton, Tennessee, where they met Anna Theresser Caswell and Maurice Soles and learned firsthand about the courageous acts that led to the desegregation of Clinton High School. The Clinton 12 encountered hatred and violence, which culminated in the bombing of the high school in 1958.[18] SIM members then went to Arkansas, where they met with Terrence Roberts and Carlotta Walls Lanier, two members of the Little Rock 9, who told them about the campaign to desegregate Little Rock Central High School. When the Little Rock 9 tried to enter the school they were stopped by the Arkansas National Guard and chased by a mob that threatened to lynch them.[19] SIM members spoke about their experiences, including their lack of access to higher education and their fear of deportation, and listened to the advice offered by Caswell, Soles, Roberts, and Lanier. The parallels and connections between the immigrant youth movement and the civil rights movement were apparent to the students: both challenged the institutional racism that systematically excludes educational access to youth of color.

Students at UCLA had the opportunity to learn about the philosophy of nonviolence and the history of social movements from Lawson through classes offered by the UCLA Labor Center. These classes, which Lawson has taught for more than ten years, have been a source of inspiration for undocumented Latino and Asian students. Members of IDEAS applied his lessons in their organizing campaigns on campus and in the community.

Students block the street in front of the Federal Building near the University of California, Los Angeles, on May 20, 2010. *Courtesy of Jonathan Bibriesca.*

Particularly helpful were lectures and conversations on the Nashville sit-in campaign—the undocumented students readily identified with the African American youth who had been engaged in the civil rights movement—and the farmworkers' movement. A viewing of *A Force More Powerful*, a documentary about the power of nonviolence, offered lessons that the students could apply to the undocumented immigrant movement. Perhaps even more important than the content of the class was the opportunity it offered for engaging in a dialogue about life as undocumented students.

THE RIGHT TO DREAM CAMPAIGN

The failure of the DREAM Act in 2010 forced undocumented youth to regroup. The Republican majority in Congress was blocking immigration reform, and it was almost certain that Republicans would prevent the DREAM Act from being introduced before national elections in 2012. Youth began organizing separate campaigns in their home states over the next two years. The UWD, which by 2010 was the largest network of undocumented youth in the country, and the National Immigrant Youth Alliance (NIYA), another national network, launched the Education Not Deportation (END) campaign to stop youth deportations. Many of the youth facing deportation had been apprehended as a result of a minor offense, such as driving a vehicle with a broken taillight or driving without a license. The END campaign was able to stop the majority of these deportations through public campaigns and political pressure, and ICE released many of those who had been detained.[20] In spite of these successes, each case placed a strain on the organizers and their resources. A systemic change was needed. Additionally, the majority of the victories involved individuals already connected with the movement. Many more undocumented youth were being deported because they did not know that they could challenge the system and fight their deportation.

In January 2011, Tom Saenz, president and general counsel of the Mexican American Legal Defense and Educational Fund (MALDEF), convened a meeting with undocumented youth in Southern California. Those who were present had worked tirelessly in the DREAM Act campaign, as Dominguez recalled.

There were fifty or more people who showed up that day and [Tom Saenz] gave us this motivational speech: "You've been leaders of the movement." But he also planted some seeds to think about. He said, "You have the most creative and innovative organizing we have seen in decades, so I expect you to come up with the next plan." And it was a very clear mandate. He reminded us that the legislature is not the only place with a platform to fight for our rights.[21]

By February, Dominguez had started conducting research with a small team composed of DTLA and OCDT members, attorneys, and law students. Their goal was to develop new legal approaches.

Dominguez immigrated to the United States with her mother and younger sister at the age of nine. She grew up in Pasadena, California, and was introduced to organizing by her mother, her greatest role model. She attended the University of California, Santa Cruz, and qualified for in-state tuition under AB 540. She was shocked by the lack of support for undocumented students, even though the law had passed four years before she enrolled, and she noted that the university was "not ready to help undocumented students."[22] This lack of support led her and her classmates to form Students Informing Now (SIN), a student organization to support undocumented students. After graduation she worked as an organizer for the campaign by the Community Labor Environment Action Network (CLEAN) to unionize car wash workers, the majority of whom are undocumented immigrants.

Dominguez, who currently serves as the AFL-CIO's director of labor and community partnerships, has drawn inspiration from the civil rights movement and *The Children* by David Halberstam, which chronicles the movement and Lawson's role in the Nashville sit-ins.

> Reading [*The Children*] gave me courage. There were so many similarities between those students and us, even the fears about being young. It reminded me that we certainly were not the first young people in this country to stand up for something that was righteous, and we still have a lot to learn from Reverend Lawson and others. I felt a lot of comfort in learning about their story, and they were the same ages as we were.[23]

The Children prompted Dominquez to reflect on the role of nonviolence and how oppressed people can challenge institutions that deprive communities of their dignity and humanity. It also provided the motivation she needed to continue fighting, despite the criticism and barriers faced by the undocumented youth movement. She was able to see herself and other undocumented youth in the young activists working to desegregate Nashville.

Undocumented youth continued to be deported as Dominguez and the rest the team researched strategies in early 2011. In March the third annual UWD Congress took place at the Highlander Research and Education Center in New Market, Tennessee. The Highlander Center is a historic site for the labor and civil rights movements because it was the location for workshops and training sessions that brought together a group of multiracial leaders and activists during the 1950s and 1960s. Five decades later, over two hundred undocumented youth and their allies gathered to formulate a new strategy that would not rely on the passage of major legislation. Hollis Watkins, a veteran of the civil rights movement, addressed the participants and shared his experiences as a teenager and activist with the NAACP and the SNCC. He spoke of the death threats he received and the time he spent in jail for his activism. UWD leaders discussed the importance of collective nonviolent action to strengthen the moral heart of the fight for justice and equality.

On June 17, 2011, the director of ICE, John T. Morton, issued a memo on prosecutorial discretion, indicating that the agency would not deport low-priority

The DREAM Act campaign of the last ten years,
I think, is probably **the most exciting event in
the last thirty to forty years in the United States**.
It has come almost entirely from students without papers
who have **come out from the shadows**.
So I really think that that's one of the most exciting
developments that I know about, period. You are
**illustrating many different facets of nonviolent
philosophy in theory and in practice**.
—Rev. Lawson April 2013

individuals, which included DREAM Act–eligible youth.[24] This memo established criteria for distinguishing between low-priority and high-priority cases.[25] Obama publicly proclaimed that DREAM Act–eligible youth were not being deported, but evidence from the END campaign proved otherwise. At this point, Dominguez had what she called an "epiphany."

> When I took my AP government class, they taught us how the government has three branches: executive, judicial, and legislative. We had gone through the legislative [branch] many, many times, and they had failed us. But we had never thought about a campaign where we target the president alone. We knew he could have the power alone to give relief to undocumented youth. There are three branches of government, and this is the one we haven't tried.[26]

Dominquez and the research team concluded that they needed a campaign directed at the president. The organizers completed their legal research and developed their strategy that summer. "If the president can write an executive order to declare war," Dominguez said, "then how come he can't write an executive order to stop the deportation of all undocumented youth? They can declare war in a matter of hours, and they cannot protect these people from deportation?"[27]

Attorneys from various national organizations such as MALDEF and Asian Americans Advancing Justice (AAAJ), formerly the Asian Pacific American Legal Center (APALC), corroborated the team's research findings. The DTLA and the OCDT reached out to UWD, generating conversations with UWD's national leadership.

That summer of 2011 also saw the launch of the Dream Summer program, the first national internship program for undocumented youth. Dream Summer 2011, which was sponsored by the UCLA Labor Center, was designed to continue developing the immigrant youth leaders who had emerged during the 2010 DREAM Act campaign. The goal was to increase their organizational capacity and to help them build alliances with social justice organizations across different sectors, including labor unions. Dream Summer 2011 placed 102 undocumented youth in social justice internships throughout the country.

Dream Summer opened and closed with a retreat held in Los Angeles at the UCLA Labor Center. Lawson spoke at the first retreat. He commended the interns for their work on the DREAM Act campaign and offered advice for the future of the movement. He encouraged them to continue to organize, saying, "Only through building a mass movement will we be able to achieve meaningful immigration reform." Dominguez was a featured speaker and facilitator at the closing retreat. She led the group in a power analysis and a vigorous discussion about the research and strategy needed to push for administrative relief. The Dream Summer interns agreed to take what they had learned to their local organizations and networks.

Activists were still reeling from the failure of the DREAM Act a few months before, and at first some were skeptical of the new strategy. During the following months, the proposal was presented to as many groups as possible through webinars, phone calls, and in-person presentations. These sessions focused on why the president should be the target of the campaign. The campaign for administrative relief was gaining momentum, but the organizers wanted a better slogan. On October 2011 the name of the campaign was changed to The Right to Dream. This new name provided a sense of hope and, more important, put a human face to the campaign. Through social media, new creative slogans began to expand the scope of "the right to dream": "the right to live with my loved ones," "the right to travel safely," "the right to work," "the right to an education." People were asked to share their own slogans and photos on social media, and the campaign generated support from new allies.

The Right to Dream campaign began on October 12, 2011, when five undocumented youth—Dominguez, Meza, Francisco Bravo, Adrian González, and Tony Ortuño—held a sit-in at the office of ICE's chief prosecutor in downtown Los Angeles. The protesters called on Obama to end the deportation of undocumented youth by using his executive power to provide administrative relief. Over one hundred undocumented youth, allies, and community members held a rally outside the ICE offices to support the five who were risking arrest. Dominguez recalls, "I was handcuffed, but I felt the most powerful ever. Because there was

Ju Hong and other undocumented students stage a protest against US immigration policy in August 2011 in San Bernardino, California. *Courtesy of Ju Hong.*

nothing else left. If I was ever going to be arrested, I always thought it had better to be under my own terms and that's exactly what happened."[28]

The civil disobedience action came at a very difficult time for Dominguez. Her stepfather, who strongly backed the undocumented youth movement and was one of her greatest supporters, was battling cancer. Dominguez said that he participated in the protest despite great discomfort.

> Raul was still in very much pain, but he and my mom came out to the action. As I was sitting inside the ICE chief prosecutor's office, Raul was in tremendous pain. But he was there, and he was one of the loudest chanters. Seven days later he ended up in the hospital, and a month and a half later, he passed away.[29]

Although this was a tragic time in Dominguez's life, the death of her stepfather strengthened her motivation to continue fighting for administrative action.

Following the sit-in, Meza and three other UWD representatives—Erika Andiola from Arizona, Matias Ramos from California, and Carlos Saavedra from Massachusetts—met with Cecilia Muñoz, former White House director of intergovernmental affairs and Obama's top immigration advisor, and other White House staff to discuss the possibility of the president stopping the deportation of undocumented youth. The immigrant youth presented their research and suggested ways the president might take action. The White House representatives were neither encouraging nor supportive, and Obama publicly claimed that he did not have the legal authority to make this change.

Although the campaign had gained some momentum among immigrant youth, the administration continued to deport thousands of people daily and it seemed at times that the campaign would not succeed. Not all immigrant youth were on board, and the immigrant rights organizations were dismissive. In addition, the presidential primaries were coming up, and anti-immigrant sentiment was intensifying as Republican candidates vied for conservative voters.

In an attempt to court Latinos to the Republican Party, Florida senator Marco Rubio proposed a bill that was similar to the DREAM Act. Although it did not provide a pathway to citizenship, it addressed all the other the demands made by the Right to Dream campaign. This provided political leverage that could be applied to the Obama administration. Amador, a key organizer of the Right to Dream campaign, explained the importance of Rubio's proposed legislation.

> Senator Marco Rubio . . . came out saying that he would be introducing a DREAM-like bill that was going to provide essentially what we were asking for, but through legislative avenues. This threatened the Democrats and the president. UWD, who were part of the campaign, said we were open to having conversations with Senator Rubio. This opened the doors to the White House, who began calling UWD and asking if immigrant youth were really going to meet with him. That is the point when meetings started getting serious.[30]

Amador noted that the Right to Dream campaign team stressed that Obama could lose the Latino vote if he did not take action.

> Putting it into a political context, we used those announcements, those actions to our favor. We were framing the message that President Obama needs to act on this because he needs the Latino vote. He needs to deliver because of his horrible record on deportations. He needs to deliver a victory to energize the left. We needed to play the game with the cards we had.[31]

Neidi Dominguez is arrested for participating in a sit-in at the ICE offices in Los Angeles, October 12, 2011. *Courtesy of Adrian Sanchez.*

The campaign team decided that the most effective way to persuade the Obama administration to provide relief would not involve mobilizing thousands of people to march in the streets—the primary tactic of the 2010 campaign. Instead, organizers would focus on delivering their message through the media. The framing of the message and the use of social and mainstream media would have to be disciplined and on point.

A second legal team was created on the East Coast, and Dominguez shared the findings from the research that had been conducted in Los Angeles. Hiroshi Motomura, a UCLA law professor, was asked to assist the research committee in Los Angeles. He drafted a letter that was presented at a meeting between legal experts and immigrant youth organizers, which took place at the UCLA Labor Center in early May. It was cosigned by ninety-eight law professors from all over the country, and he sent it to Obama on May 28, 2012. The letter rebuked the president's claim that he lacked the authority to provide administrative relief, stating that the president has "clear executive authority for several forms of administrative relief for Dream Act beneficiaries."[32]

Within days the UWD received a call from White House officials, who asked to meet with members of the campaign team. Dominguez, Lorella Praeli from Connecticut, and Gaby Pacheco from Florida, representing UWD, along with five attorneys from the Los Angeles and East Coast legal teams, met with White House staff. The meeting could not be held inside the White House because some of the organizers were barred from entering because of their immigration status. During the meeting the team presented the demands of the Right to Dream campaign and gave the administration a deadline of June 12 for the president's response. If the deadline was not met, immigrant youth were ready to take action in the swing states with large Latino populations, such as Colorado, New Mexico, and Florida.

Organizers with the NIYA were also engaged in strategic discussions about how to end the deportation of DREAM Act–eligible youth. They decided to stage civil disobedience actions at the Obama for America (OFA) campaign offices, where they would demand administrative relief. Luis Serrano, at that time a member of the NIYA, recalled that he heard about the Right to Dream campaign while the NIYA was discussing its options for direct action. The NIYA continued to receive information about Right to Dream as they made the decision to take over the OFA offices.[33] NIYA leaders Mateo, Abdollahi, and Jonathan Perez developed training to prepare immigrant youth for the nonviolent action.[34] They were unaware of the meeting that the UWD had with White House staff and the deadline that had been given to Obama.

On June 5, seven days before the deadline, two undocumented youth, Javier Hernandez and Veronica Gomez, held a six-day sit-in and hunger strike inside the OFA office in Denver. Denver police chose not to arrest them. Instead, the Obama campaign staff closed the office and let Hernandez and Gomez stay overnight. The NIYA organizers saw this as a victory. The OFA did not want to have these youth arrested because it would generate bad press, and with the office closed, staff and volunteers could not come in and the campaign could not solicit contributions.[35] NIYA organizers issued a press statement calling for Obama to immediately end the deportation of undocumented youth and to grant them administrative relief. The press statement also encouraged immigrant youth groups to take action. OFA offices in California, Colorado, Georgia, Michigan and North Carolina were also shut down by undocumented youth who held sit-ins and called for the president to respond.[36] Lawson reflected on these actions:

> Going after the campaign offices for the reelection of the president was really a stroke of genius. And it did not require in those instances a mass meeting, a mass movement. It only required a few disciplined people going to his

campaign offices. What do you do about that group of students? Do you arrest them and cause massive publicity because you arrested them? Well, then that would harm your reelection efforts with the Latino community and lots of other communities. So, what do you do? Do you just let them sit? Then you can't do your work. You are paralyzed. So that forced the president to say, "Who said I don't have the authority?," and his lawyers, who said, "We cannot do it," to change their minds and do it.[37]

White House staff called UWD to find out why people were taking over the OFA offices before the June 12 deadline. After that call, the White House broke off communication with the UWD.

The second Dream Summer internship program began that weekend in Los Angeles. On June 14, Dominguez trained over 120 interns for a direct action in front of the Federal building in downtown Los Angeles, which would begin the escalation of the campaign. The next day, as the action in front of the Federal building was underway, Janet Napolitano, secretary of the US Department of Homeland Security (DHS), made the following announcement.

> Effective immediately, certain young people who were brought to the United States as young children, do not present a risk to national security or public safety, and meet several key criteria will be considered for relief from removal from the country or from entering into removal proceedings. Those who demonstrate that they meet the criteria will be eligible to receive deferred action for a period of two years, subject to renewal, and will be eligible to apply for work authorization.[38]

Dream Summer protestors block an entrance to the Hollywood Freeway in Los Angeles on June 15, 2012, shortly before the Deferred Action for Childhood Arrivals (DACA) program is announced. *Courtesy of Adrian Sanchez.*

Following Napolitano's announcement, Obama expressed his support for the new DHS policy in televised remarks.

In spite of the euphoria that greeted the president's comments, undocumented youth were skeptical. There was a sense of disbelief. Immigrant youth were wary of the words of a president who had failed the immigrant community by deporting the largest number of people in US history. The students also mistrusted the DHS, which had previously issued memos advising that deportations be treated as a low priority but had failed to enforce this policy.

When the DACA program was announced in 2012, new challenges emerged for the immigrant youth movement. In the following months, activists mobilized throughout the country to recruit and teach undocumented youth how to prepare their DACA applications. On August 15, 2012, US Citizenship and Immigrations Services (USCIS) released the application forms. During the following months undocumented youth groups and immigrant, community, and service organizations set up free clinics to provide information and legal assistance to thousands of prospective applicants. The DACA clinics were essential, reaching thousands of undocumented youth who had never heard of the DREAM Act, who could not afford college, and who were unaware that other undocumented youth were fighting for their rights.

The DACA clinics provided advice to applicants who could not afford an attorney and protected applicants from fraudulent notaries and lawyers who charged students for the applications, which were available for free online, and charged exorbitant fees to process them.[39] At some DACA clinics immigrant youth camped out the night before the applications

Neidi Dominguez (center) speaks to the press in Los Angeles after the announcement of the Deferred Action for Childhood Arrivals (DACA) program on June 15, 2012. *Courtesy of Adrian Sanchez.*

were available and waited in line for hours to apply. Fear that DACA would be rescinded if Obama were not reelected heightened the urgency that many felt. Task forces were put together in various cities to coordinate the efforts of organizations that could assist applicants. Some scholarships were made available to support those who could not afford the filing fees. At the national level various organizations came together to develop a website called *Own the Dream*, a hub of resources to help undocumented youth apply for DACA. The DACA clinics also recruited more immigrant youth to join the movement.

By February 2014, the USCIS had approved 610,694 DACA applications.[40] Hundreds of thousands of lives have been fundamentally altered by the dedication and courage of a few immigrant youth organizers and allies. Although it is a temporary solution, DACA has provided hope to many immigrants who continue to live in the shadows.

THE JOURNEY TOWARD EQUALITY

Since the DACA victory in 2012, the focus of the undocumented youth movement has changed. Access to higher education is no longer the central issue for many undocumented youth. Activists have expanded the movement to be more inclusive of the broader needs of the immigrant community. The narrative of the successful Dreamer, which was effective in gaining support for the DREAM Act, established a false dichotomy between the "good immigrant" and the "bad immigrant." Statements such as "these young people came to the US through no fault of our own" could imply that the parents are to blame for bringing their children to this country. The Dreamer narrative also excluded hundreds of thousands of immigrant youth for whom education is not an option because of structural barriers such as a lack of in-state tuition or financial aid and the need to enter the workforce to support their families.

Messages that emphasize the importance of immigrant families have tended to focus on heterosexual families, excluding LGBTQ immigrants. "Undocuqueer" youth who want to promote their queer identity as they campaign for legal status have been discouraged by some immigrant rights advocates who do not want to offend conservative groups and traditional religious institutions. Gutierrez, a leading undocuqueer organizer and a hunger strike participant, reflected on the need to challenge mainstream ideas that silence LGBTQ undocumented youth.

> We cannot make the mistake that other social justice movements have made, which is [to] erase the contributions of groups of people that have played a pivotal role in our movements. LGBTQ undocumented youth, or "undocuqueers," have been at the forefront of the immigrant youth movement since its beginning. We have been present in the strategy making, risking arrest and deportation, and taking over the streets, but our presence and contribution has not always been explicit.[41]

Many undocuqueer organizers and allies find inspiration from the work of civil rights leader Bayard Rustin, who was gay.[42] Rustin was one of King's close allies and the lead organizer of the historic 1963 march on Washington, DC. Like today's undocuqueer youth, Rustin was persecuted for his sexual identity.[43]

Undocumented Asian and Pacific Islander (API) youth have also expanded the scope of the immigrant youth movement by challenging the marginalization of the API community in the immigrant discourse, which has resulted in a lack of resources and support.[44] The immigration issue is frequently seen as a Latino-only issue. Undocumented youth are creating ways to be inclusive of others and to ensure that their intersecting identities are reflected in the movement.

Seth Ronquillo and Ilse Escobar participate in a civil disobedience action outside the Los Angeles Metropolitan Detention Center in December 2013. *Courtesy of Adrian Gonzalez.*

ADVANCING EQUALITY FOR THE IMMIGRANT COMMUNITY

Undocumented youth captured the attention of the nation and advanced educational rights, justice, and equality for the immigrant community. By declaring themselves undocumented and unafraid, risking arrest and deportation, engaging in civil disobedience, and organizing hunger strikes and rallies, undocumented youth came to recognize their own power to create social change. Leaders and organizers with the immigrant youth movement see that the fight for immigrant rights is part of a greater fight for social justice. Nonviolence has played an elemental role in these accomplishments.

The movement that was launched in an effort to pass the DREAM Act eventually forged connections across other movements and causes that address labor rights, LGBTQ rights, access to health care and education, and the problem of mass incarceration. The victory represented by the DACA program could not have been achieved without the commitment of immigrant youth. The innovative tactics of the youth organizers and their firm belief in the power of nonviolence were essential to the implementation of DACA. The undocumented youth movement has energized the immigration debate, built a model of nonviolent direct action, and changed the course of US immigration history.

NOTES

This chapter draws extensively from interviews of Rev. Lawson and guest speakers that were held during a special topics course sponsored by the Labor Center, the César E. Chávez Department of Chicana/o Studies, the Labor and Workplace Studies Minor, the Department of African American Studies, and the History Department at UCLA.

1. Federal Bureau of Prisons, "Population Statistics," 2013, http://www.bop.gov/about/statistics /population_statistics.jsp.

2. Immigration Policy Center, "Who and Where the DREAMers Are: A Demographic Profile of Immigrants Who Might Benefit from the Obama Administration's Deferred Action Initiative," American Immigration Council website, July 2012, http://www.immigrationpolicy.org/sites/default/files/docs/who _and_where_the_dreamers_are_0.pdf.

3. DACA regularized the status of an estimated three million undocumented people. See Gabriela Madera et al., *Underground Undergrads: UCLA Undocumented Immigrant Students Speak Out* (Los Angeles: UCLA Center for Labor Research and Education, 2008), 3.

4. Ibid., 2.

5. Ibid., 3.

6. Ibid., 15.

7. National Conference of State Legislatures, "Undocumented Student Tuition State Action," June 12, 2014, National Conference of State Legislatures website, http://www.ncsl.org/research/education /undocumented-student-tuition-state-action.aspx.

8. Ibid.

9. Ibid.

10. Carlos Amador, "This is Our Country Too: Undocumented Immigrant Youth Organizing and the Battle for the DREAM Act," *Critical Planning: UCLA Urban Planning Journal* 18 (2011): 112.

11. Kent Wong et al., *Undocumented and Unafraid: Tam Tran, Cynthia Felix, and the Immigrant Youth Movement* (Los Angeles: UCLA Center for Labor Research and Education, 2012), 57.

12. David Halberstam, *The Children* (New York: Random House, 1998), 217–18, 506–7.

13. Neidi Dominguez, James M. Lawson Jr., Carlos Amador, and Sofia Campos, interview by Kent Wong, April 24, 2013, Los Angeles.

14. Amador, "This Is Our Country Too," 114.

15. Ibid.

16. Dominguez, Lawson, Amador, and Campos, interview by Wong.

17. Wong et al., *Undocumented and Unafraid*, 61–62.

18. Ibid.

19. Ibid.

20. National Immigrant Youth Alliance, "END Campaign," http://theniya.org/ourwork/end _campaign/index.html (no longer available).

21. Ibid.

22. Dominguez, Lawson, Amador, and Campos, interview by Wong.

23. Ibid.

24. US Immigration and Customs Enforcement, "Exercising Prosecutorial Discretion Consistent with the Civil Immigration Enforcement Priorities of the Agency for the Apprehension, Detention, and Removal of Aliens" (memorandum, June 17, 2011), US Immigration and Customs Enforcement website, http://www.ice.gov/doclib/secure-communities/pdf/prosecutorial-discretion-memo.pdf.

25. According to the USCIS, high priority cases are those who "pose a clear risk to national security; serious felons, repeat offenders, or individuals with a lengthy criminal record of any kind; known gang members or other individuals who pose a clear danger to public safety; and individuals with an egregious record of immigration violations, including those with a record of illegal re-entry and those who have engaged in immigration fraud." Low priority cases include "veterans and members of the US armed forces; long-time lawful permanent residents; minors and elderly individuals; individuals present in the United States since childhood; pregnant or nursing women; victims of domestic violence; trafficking, or other serious crimes; individuals who suffer from a serious mental or physical disability; and individuals with serious health conditions." Immigration and Customs Enforcement, "Exercising Prosecutorial Discretion."

26. Dominguez, Lawson, Amador, and Campos, interview by Wong.

27. Ibid.

28. Ibid.

29. Ibid.

30. Ibid.

31. Ibid.

32. Hiroshi Motomura, letter to President Barak Obama, May 28, 2012, www.nilc.org/document .html?id=754.

33. Luis Serrano, personal communication with author, February 2014.

34. Ibid.

35. Ibid.

36. Ibid.

37. Ibid.

38. US Department of Homeland Security, "Secretary Napolitano Announces Deferred Action Process for Young People Who Are Low Enforcement Priorities" (press release), June 15, 2012, US Department of Homeland Security website, http://www.dhs.gov/news/2012/06/15/secretary-napolitano -announces-deferred-action-process-young-people-who-are-low.

39. US Citizenship and Immigration Services, "Consideration of Deferred Action for Childhood Arrivals (DACA)," US Citizenship and Immigration Services website, http://www.uscis.gov/humanitarian /consideration-deferred-action-childhood-arrivals-daca.

40. US Citizenship and Immigration Services, "Number of I821D, Consideration of Deferred Action for Childhood Arrivals by Fiscal Year, Quarter, Intake, Biometrics and Case Status" (table), February 6, 2014, US Citizenship and Immigration Services website, http://www.uscis.gov/sites/default/files/USCIS /Resources/Reports%20and%20Studies/Immigration%20F orms%20Data/All%20Form%20Types/DACA /DACA-06-02-14.pdf.

41. Jorge Gutierrez, personal communication with author, February 2014.

42. Halberstam, *The Children*, 450.

43. Wong, *Undocumented and Unafraid*, 93–94.

44. Ibid., 96–98.

45. Dominguez, Lawson, Amador, and Campos, interview by Wong.

BIBLIOGRAPHY

Ackerman, Peter, and Jack Duvall. *A Force More Powerful: A Century of Nonviolent Conflict.* New York: Palgrave, 2000.

———. "The Nashville Sit-in Movement." *A Force More Powerful.* DVD. Directed by Steve York. Washington DC: York Zimmerman Inc., 2000.

Acuña, Rodolfo. *Anything But Mexican: Chicanos in Contemporary Los Angeles.* New York: Verso, 1996.

Amador, Carlos. 2011. "This Is Our Country Too: Undocumented Immigrant Youth Organizing and the Battle for the DREAM Act." *Critical Planning: UCLA Urban Planning Journal* 18 (2011): 110–17.

Araiza, Lauren. "Complicating the Beloved Community: The Student Nonviolent Coordinating Committee and the National Farm Workers Association." In *The Struggle in Black and Brown: African American and Mexican American Relations during the Civil Rights Era,* edited by Brian D. Benken, 78–103. Lincoln: University of Nebraska Press, 2011.

Arsenault, Raymond. *Freedom Riders: 1961 and the Struggle for Racial Justice.* New York: Oxford University Press, 2006.

Baker, Bob. "Arrests Fan Hotel's Labor Dispute." *Los Angeles Times,* October 18, 1989. http://articles.latimes.com/1989-10-18/local/me-362_1_hotel-workers.

———. "Korean Firm Fires Staff in Hyatt Wilshire Takeover." *Los Angeles Times,* January 1, 1992. http://articles.latimes.com/1992-01-01/local/e-1092_1_hyatt-workers.

———. "Union, Hyatt Hotels Still at Odds." *Los Angeles Times,* July 23, 1991. http://articles. latimes.com/1991-07-23/local/me-294_1_employee-work-schedules.

Baldwin, Lewis V., and Aprille V. Woodson. *Freedom Is Never Free: A Biographical Portrait of Edgar Daniel Nixon.* Nashville: Office of Minority Affairs, Tennessee General Assembly and Tennessee State University; Montgomery: Alabama State University, 1992.

Bardacke, Frank. "Book Talk: Trampling Out the Vintage." Paper presented at the UCLA Institute for Labor and Employment, Los Angeles, May 8, 2013.

———. *Trampling Out the Vintage: Cesar Chavez and the Two Souls of the United Farm Workers.* New York: Verso Books, 2011.

Barta, Russell. "The Domestic Worker: An Occupational Type." Master's thesis, Loyola University Chicago, 1947. Loyala eCommons, http://ecommons.luc.edu/luc_theses/44.

Batalova, Jeanne, and Margie McHugh. *DREAM vs. Reality: An Analysis of Potential DREAM Act Beneficiaries.* Washington, DC: Migration Policy Institute, 2010. www.migrationpolicy.org/pubs/DREAM-Insight-July2010.pdf.

Bondurant, Joan V. *Conquest of Violence: The Gandhian Philosophy of Conflict*. Princeton, NJ: Princeton University Press, 1958.

Brinkley, Douglas. *Rosa Parks*. New York: Viking, 2000.

Brodkin, Karen. "The Context of Labor and Immigrant Workers: Rights Activism in Los Angeles." In *Making Democracy Matter: Identity and Activism in Los Angeles*, 17–42. New Brunswick, NJ: Rutgers University Press, 2007.

"California University Workers Hold Hunger Strike." *Democracy Now!*, November 16, 1998. Radio and television news program. http://www.democracynow.org/1998/11/16 /california_university_workers_hold_ hunger_strike.

Carson, Claybourne. *In Struggle: SNCC and the Black Awakening of the 1960s*. Cambridge, MA: Harvard University Press, 1981.

————, ed. *The Movement, 1964–1970*. Westport, CT: Greenwood Press, 1993.

Carson, Claybourne, David Garrow, Gerald Gill, Vincent Harding, and Darlene Clark Hine, eds. *The Eyes on the Prize, Civil Rights Reader: Documents, Speeches, and Firsthand Accounts from the Black Freedom Struggle*. New York: Penguin Books, 1991.

Chávez, César. *An Organizer's Tale: Speeches*. Edited by Ilan Stavans. New York: Penguin Books, 2008.

Congress of Racial Equality. "The History of CORE." Congress of Racial Equality website. http://www.core-online.org/History/history.htm.

Dalton, Frederick John. *The Moral Vision of César Chávez*. New York: Orbis Books, 2003.

"Damage of Fear and the Promise of Love, The." *The Student Voice*, 1, no. 5 (1960): 2. http://www.crmvet.org/docs/sv/sv6006.pdf.

Dickerson, Dennis. "James M. Lawson, Jr.: Methodism, Nonviolence and the Civil Rights Movement." *Methodist History* 52, no. 3 (2014): 168–86.

Doak, Robin S. *Dolores Huerta: Labor Leader and Civil Rights Activist*. Minneapolis: Compass Point Books, 2008.

Doherty, Jake. "Hotel Labor Pact: Room for Everyone." *Los Angeles Times*, November 1, 1992. http://articles.latimes.com/1992-11-01/news/ci-1937_1_wilshire-plaza-hotel.

Durazo, Maria Elena. "Fasting to Right Worker Injustices." *Los Angeles Times*, May 25, 1999. http://articles.latimes.com/1999/may/25/local/me-40625.

————. "Maria Elena Durazo: Controversial Local Union Head Takes No Prisoners to Win the Point." Interview by Steve Proffitt. *Los Angeles Times*, September 27, 1992. http://articles.latimes.com/1992-09-27/opinion/op-486_1_los-angeles.

Emery, Theo. "Activist Ousted from Vanderbilt Is Back, as a Teacher." *New York Times*, October 4, 2006. http://www.nytimes.com/2006/10/04/education/04lawson.html.

Etheridge, Eric. "James Lawson: How the Nashville Movement Kept the Riders Riding." *Breach of Peace: Portraits of the 1961 Mississippi Freedom Riders*. Website. http://breachofpeace.com/blog/?p=57.

Faith Project, Inc. "James Lawson." *This Far by Faith: African American Spiritual Journeys*. Website, 2003. http://www.pbs.org/thisfarbyfaith/witnesses/james _lawson.html.

Feingold, Danny. "Putting Faith in Labor." *Los Angeles Times*, August 28, 1998. http:// articles.latimes.com/1998/aug/28/news/ls-17211/3.

Fellowship of Recognition. "History of the Fellowship of Reconciliation." Fellowship of Recognition website. http://forusa.org/about/history.

Ferriss, Susan, and Ricardo Sandoval. *The Fight in the Fields: Cesar Chavez and the Farmworkers Movement*. Edited by Diana Hembree. New York: Harcourt Brace, 1997.

Frank, Larry, and Kent Wong. "Dynamic Political Mobilization: The Los Angeles County Federation of Labor." *WorkingUSA* 8, no. 2 (2004): 155–81.

Gandhi, Mohandas K. *An Autobiography: The Story of My Experiments with Truth.* Boston: Beacon Press, 1993.

Ganz, Marshall. *Why David Sometimes Wins: Leadership, Organization, and Strategy in the California Farm Worker Movement.* New York: Oxford University Press, 2010.

Geron, Kim. "Hotel Workers Defeat the Hyatt Touch." *Labor Notes* (Detroit), December 1991.

Goldman, John J. "2003 Freedom Ride Ends with a New York Rally." *Los Angeles Times,* October 5, 2003. http://articles.latimes.com/2003/oct/05/nation/na-freedom5.

Halberstam, David. *The Children.* New York: Random House, 1998.

Hartford, Bruce. "Freedom Rides of 1961." Veterans of the Civil Rights Movement website. http://www.crmvet.org/riders/freedom_rides.pdf.

Hernandez, Marita. "Organizer Wins Post of President: Latina Leads Takeover of Union from Anglo Males." *Los Angeles Times,* May 6, 1989. http://articles.latimes.com /1989-05-06/news/mn-2087_1_durazo-s-english-union-from-anglo-males-maria -elena-durazo.

Hondagneu-Sotelo, Pierrette. *God's Heart Has No Borders: How Religious Activists Are Working for Immigrant Rights.* Berkeley: University of California Press, 2008.

Honey, Michael K. *Going Down Jericho Road: The Memphis Strike, Martin Luther King's Last Campaign.* New York: Norton, 2007.

Hong, Peter Y. "Fasting Union Leader Asks City Council to Influence USC." *Los Angeles Times,* May 19, 1999. http://articles.latimes.com/1999/may/19/local/me-38785.

Hoose, Phillip. *Claudette Colvin: Twice toward Justice.* New York: Farrar, Straus & Giroux, 2009.

Houston, Donna, and Laura Pulido. "The Work of Performativity: Staging Social Justice at the University of California." In *Critical Theories, Radical Pedagogies, and Global Conflicts,* edited by Gustavo Fishman, 317–42. Oxford: Rowman and Littlefield, 2005.

Immigration Policy Center. "Who and Where the DREAMers Are." American Immigration Council website, July 2012. http://www.immigrationpolicy.org/sites/default/files /docs/who_and_where_the_d reamers_are_0.pdf.

Isaac, Larry. "Movement of Movements: Culture Moves in the Long Civil Rights Struggle." *Social Forces* 87, no. 1 (2008): 33–63.

Janis-Aparicio, Madeline, Steve Cancian, and Gary Phillips. "Building a Movement for a Living Wage." *Poverty and Race* 5, no. 1 (1996): 33–63. http://www.prrac.org /full_text.php?text_id=371&item_id=3673&newsletter_id=24 &header=Poverty +%2F+Welfare.

Kamin, Ben. *Room 306: The National Story of the Lorraine Motel.* East Lansing: Michigan State University Press, 2012.

Kang, K. Connie. "UCLA Class Puts Theory to Test in the Real World." *Los Angeles Times,* March 11, 1995. http://articles.latimes.com/1995-03-11/local/me-41292_1_asian -american-studies.

Kelley, Blair L. M. *Right to Ride: Streetcar Boycotts and African American Citizenship in the Era of Plessy v. Ferguson.* Chapel Hill: University of North Carolina Press, 2010.

King, Martin Luther, Jr. "I've Been to the Mountaintop." Speech, Memphis, April 3, 1968. King Papers, Martin Luther King Jr. Research and Education Institute, Stanford University. Website. http://mlk-kpp01.stanford.edu/index.php/encyclopedia /documentsentry/ive_been_to_the_mountaintop.

———. "MIA Mass Meeting at Holt Street Baptist Church." Speech, Montgomery, December 5, 1955. King Papers, Martin Luther King Jr. Research and Education Institute,

Stanford University. Website. http://mlk-kpp01.stanford.edu/kingweb/publications /papers/vol3/551205.004-MIA_Mass_Meeting_at_Holt_Street_Baptist_Church.htm.

———. "Statement on Ending the Bus Boycott." Speech, Montgomery, December 20, 1956. King Papers, Martin Luther King Jr. Research and Education Institute, Stanford University. Website. https://kinginstitute.stanford.edu/king-papers/documents /statement-ending-bus-boycott.

———. *Stride toward Freedom: The Montgomery Story.* New York: Harper & Brothers, 1958.

———. "Testimony in State of Alabama v. M. L. King, Jr." Trial transcript, Montgomery, March 19–22, 1956. King Papers, Martin Luther King Jr. Research and Education Institute, Stanford Library. Website. https://kinginstitute.stanford.edu/kingpapers /documents/testimony-state-alabama-v-m-l-king-jr.

Konley, Patricia, compiler. "Platform: 'Leaders Must Be Willing to Take Risks, Sacrifice.'" *Los Angeles Times,* November 22, 1993. http://articles.latimes.com/1993-11-22 /local/me-59560_1_leader.

"Latina Will Head Hotel Workers Union." *Los Angeles Times,* April 21, 1989. http://articles. latimes.com/1989-04-21/local/me-2227_1_hotel-and-restaurant-workers-maria -elena-durazo-restaurant-employees-union.

Lawson, James M., Jr. "A Comparative View of the Nonviolent System from Three Perspectives." Handout, undated. Private collection.

———. "A Conversation with James Lawson." YouTube video, 23:45. Posted by WPNT, Nashville Public Television, November 9, 2009. http://www.youtube.com /watch?v=8SMLebhfPE8.

———. Interview by Robert Penn Warren, March 17, 1964. Transcript, Robert Penn Warren Civil Rights Oral History Project, University of Kentucky Special Collections, Lexington.

———. "Interview: Rev. James Lawson." *Nashville 1960: We Were Warriors.* Part 1 of *A Force More Powerful: A Century of Nonviolent Conflict.* Broadcast on PBS, September 18, 2000. http://web.archive.org/web/20041209111131 /http://www.pbs.org/weta/forcem orepowerful/nashville/interview.html.

———. "James Lawson—Gandhi and Nonviolence." YouTube video, 3:36. Posted by International Center on Nonviolent Conflict, September 30, 2010. http://www.youtube.com/watch?v=Q8K4HLM03dw.

———. "James M. Lawson Jr." *Robert Penn Warren's "Who Speaks for the Negro": An Archival Collection.* Website. http://whospeaks.library.vanderbilt.edu/interview /james-m-lawson-jr.

———. "Nashville Sit-in Movement." Lecture, University of California, Los Angeles, January 23, 2013.

———. "The Nonviolent Method (as Taught from the 1950s with Great Indebtedness to Gandhi and the Nonviolent Movement, 1955–1975)." Handout, 2001 Private collection.

———. "The Philosophy of Nonviolence." Lecture, University of California, Los Angeles, January 9 and April 17, 2013.

———. "Seeking First the Kingdom: The Nashville Story, 1958–1962." Cole Lecture, October 15, 2009. YouTube video, 1:38:33. Posted by Vanderbilt University, October 19, 2009. http://www.youtube.com/watch?v=whSYy1Iy-HI.

Lee, Barry Everett. "The Nashville Civil Rights Movement: A Study of the Phenomenon of Intentional Leadership Development and Its Consequences for Local Movements and the National Civil Rights Movement." PhD dissertation, Georgia State

University, 2010. http://scholarworks.gsu.edu/cgi/viewcontent.cgi?article=1015 &con text=history_diss.

Lewis, John. *Walking with the Wind: A Memoir of the Movement.* New York: Simon and Schuster, 1998.

Limbo, Ernest M. "James Lawson: The Nashville Civil Rights Movement." In *The Human Tradition in the Civil Rights Movement,* edited by Susan M. Glisson, 157–80. Lanham, MD: Roman and Littlefield, 2006.

"Little Strike That Grew to La Causa, The." *Time,* July 4, 1969, 16–21.

Litwack, Leon F. "Hellhounds." In *Without Sanctuary: Lynching Photography in America,* edited by James Allen, 8–37. Santa Fe: Twin Palms Publishers, 2000.

———. *Trouble in Mind: Black Southerners in the Age of Jim Crow.* New York: Alfred A. Knopf, 1998.

Mabalon, Dawn. *Little Manila Is In the Heart.* Durham, NC: Duke University Press, 2013.

Madera, Gabriela, Angelo A. Mathay, Armin M. Najafi, Hector H. Saldivar, Stephanie Solis, Alyssa Jane M. Titong, Gaspar Rivera-Salgado, Janna Shadduck-Hernandez, Kent Wong, Rebecca Frazier, and Julie Monroe. *Underground Undergrads: UCLA Undocumented Immigrant Students Speak Out.* Los Angeles: UCLA Center for Labor Research and Education, 2008.

Malnic, Eric. "Hotel Accepts Union, Will Rehire Workers." *Los Angeles Times,* October 23, 1992. http://articles.latimes.com/1992-10-23/local/me-676_1_wilshire-plaza -hotel.

Marable, Manning. *The Third Reconstruction: Black Nationalism and Race Relations after the Revolution.* Dayton: Black Research Associates, 1980.

McDonnell, Patrick J. "37 Protesters Arrested in Hotel Labor Dispute." *Los Angeles Times,* December 2, 1994. http://articles.latimes.com/1994-12-02/local/me-4183 _1_union-contract.

McGuire, Danielle L. "At the Dark End of the Street: Sexualized Violence, Community Mobilization, and the African American Freedom Struggle." PhD dissertation, Rutgers University, 2007.

Murray, Bobbi. *Arcing toward Justice: The Evolution of the Living Wage Movement.* San Francisco: Tides Foundation, 2002. http://www.tides.org/fileadmin/user/pdf /TidesFoundation_ArcingTowardJustice.pdf.

———. "Living Wage Come of Age: An Increasingly Sophisticated Movement Has Put Opponents on the Defensive." *The Nation,* July 23, 2001.

———. "Organize! Living Wage Lives in LA." *Shelterforce,* January/February 1998. http://www.nhi.org/online/issues/97/organize.html.

Nashville Christian Leadership Council. *Toward the Beloved Community: Story of the Nashville Christian Leadership Council.* Nashville: Nashville Christian Leadership Council, 1961. crmvet.org, http://www.crmvet.org/docs/61_nclc.pdf.

National Conference of State Legislatures. *Undocumented Student Tuition: State Action.* National Conference of State Legislatures website, June 12, 2014. http://www.ncsl .org/research/education/undocumented-student-tuition-state-action.aspx.

NBC News. "NBC News Special: White Paper: Sit-In." NBC broadcast, December 20, 1960. http://www.nbcuniversalarchives.com/nbcuni/clip/51A02201_s01.do.

"Negroes Press Protest in South, but the Cold Limits Activities." *New York Times,* March 4, 1960.

New Los Angeles, The. DVD. Directed by Lyn Goldfarb. Berkeley, CA: Berkeley Media, 2005.

Olivas, Michael A. "The Political Economy of the DREAM Act and the Legislative Process:

A Case Study of Comprehensive Immigration Reform." *Wayne Law Review* 55 (2010): 1757–1810.

Oshinsky, David M. "Freedom Riders." *New York Times*, March 15, 1998. http://www.nytimes.com/books/98/03/15/reviews/980315.15oshinst.html?_r=1.

Parks, Rosa, with James Haskins. *Rosa Parks: My Story*. New York: Dial Books, 1992.

Patler, Caitlin, and Lauren D. Appelbaum. *Reaching the Dream: The Federal DREAM Act, the California Dream Act, and Undocumented Student Activism*. Research and Policy Brief No. 10. Los Angeles: UCLA Institute for Research on Labor and Employment, 2011.

Pawel, Miriam. *The Union of Their Dreams: Power, Hope, and Struggle in Cesar Chavez's Farm Worker Movement*. New York: Bloomsbury Press, 2009.

Payne, Charles M. *I've Got the Light of Freedom: The Organizing Tradition and the Mississippi Freedom Struggle*. Berkeley: University of California Press, 1995.

Perman, Michael. *Struggle for Mastery: Disenfranchisement in the South, 1888–1908*. Chapel Hill: University of North Carolina Press, 2001.

Prouty, Marco G. *César Chávez, the Catholic Bishops, and the Farmworkers' Struggle for Social Justice*. Tucson: University Arizona Press, 2006.

Pulido, Laura. "The Roots of Political Consciousness among Militant Unionists and Worker Activists in Los Angeles." Paper. Southern California Studies Center, University of Southern California, February 1998. http://www.usc.edu/dept/LAS/SC2/pdf/pulido.pdf.

Reynolds, David. "The Living Wage Movement Sweeps the Nation." *WorkingUSA* 3, no. 3 (1999): 61–80.

Ritterhouse, Jennifer L. *Growing Up Jim Crow: How Black and White Southern Children Learned Race*. Chapel Hill: University of North Carolina Press, 2006.

Rivera Brooks, Nancy. "Hyatt Touch Leaves Labor Touchy." *Los Angeles Times*, September 27, 1990. http://articles.latimes.com/1990-09-27/business/fi-1844_1_hyatt-hotels.

Robinson, Jo Ann. *The Montgomery Bus Boycott and the Women Who Started It: The Memoir of Jo Ann Gibson Robinson*. Edited by David J. Garrow. Knoxville: University of Tennessee Press, 1987.

Rorlich, Ted. "USC Workers Launch Fast in Job Dispute." *Los Angeles Times*, November 19, 1998. http://articles.latimes.com/1998/nov/19/local/me-44442.

Rose, Margaret. "Women in the United Farm Workers: A Study of Chicana and Mexicana Participation in a Labor Union, 1950–1980," PhD dissertation, University of California, Los Angeles, 1988.

Scharlin, Craig, and Lilia Villanueva. *Philip Vera Cruz: A Personal History of Filipino Immigrants and the Farmworkers Movement*. Washington: University of Washington Press, 2000.

Shaw, Randy. *Beyond the Fields: Cesar Chavez, the UFW, and the Struggle for Justice in the 21st Century*. Berkeley: University of California Press, 2008.

Sipchen, Bob. "Labor of Love." *Los Angeles Times*, March 9, 1997. http://articles.latimes.com/1997-03-09/news/ls-36265_1_labor-movement.

Sitton, Claude. "Negro Sitdowns Stir Fear of Wider Unrest in the South." *New York Times*, February 14, 1960. http://www.nytimes.com/learning/general/onthisday/big/0201.html.

Slessarev-Jamir, Helene. *Prophetic Activism: Progressive Religious Justice Movements in Contemporary America*. New York: New York University Press, 2011.

Smith, Kelly Miller. Interview by Robert Penn Warren, February 13, 1964. Transcript, Robert Penn Warren Civil Rights Oral History Project, University of Kentucky Special Collections, Lexington.

———. "Kelly Miller Smith." *Robert Penn Warren's "Who Speaks for the Negro": An Archival Collection*. Website. http://whospeaks.library.vanderbilt.edu/interview/kelly -miller-smith.

"SNCC Conference." *The Student Voice* 1, no. 3 (1960): 1. http://www.crmvet.org/docs/sv /sv6010.pdf.

Stollman, Jennifer A. "Diane Nash: 'Courage Displaces Fear, Love Transforms Hate': Civil Rights Activism and the Commitment to Nonviolence." In *The Human Tradition in the Civil Rights Movement*, edited by Susan M. Glisson, 199–218. Lanham, MD: Roman and Littlefield, 2006.

Stuart, Forrest. "From the Shop to the Streets: UNITE HERE Organizing in Los Angeles Hotels." In *Working for Justice: The L.A. Model of Organizing and Advocacy,* edited by Ruth Milkman, Joshua Bloom, and Victor Narro, 194–210. New York: Cornell University Press, 2010.

Tolnay, Stewart E., and E. M. Beck. *Festival of Violence: An Analysis of Southern Lynching, 1882–1930*. Champaign: University of Illinois Press, 1995.

United Press International. "Divinity Dean Out in Racial Protest: Vanderbilt University Aide Resigns Over Refusal to Readmit Negro Student." *New York Times*, May 31, 1960.

UNITE HERE Local 11. *City on the Edge*. YouTube video, 12:36. Posted by uniteherevideos, September 21, 2010. https://www.youtube.com/watch?v=i6gDA0Agh3M.

US Citizenship and Immigration Services. "Consideration of Deferred Action for Childhood Arrivals (DACA)." US Citizenship and Immigration Services website, accessed Februrary 2014. http://www.uscis.gov/humanitarian/consideration-deferred -action-childhood-arrivals-daca.

US Department of Homeland Security. "Secretary Napolitano Announces Deferred Action Process for Young People Who Are Low Enforcement Priorities." Press release, June 15, 2012. US Immigration and Customs Enforcement website. https://www.dhs.gov/news/2012/06/15/secretary-napolitano-announces-deferred -action-process-young-people-who-are-low.

US Immigration and Customs Enforcement. "Exercising Prosecutorial Discretion Consistent with the Civil Immigration Enforcement Priorities of the Agency for Apprehension, Detention, and Removal of Aliens." Memorandum, June 17, 2011. US Immigration and Customs Enforcement website. https: www.ice.gov/.../pdf/prosecutorial -discretion-memo.pdf.

Weingroff, Richard. *The Road to Civil Rights*. Federal Highway Administration website. http://www.fhwa.dot.gov/highwayhistory/road/road.pdf.

Williams, Donnie, with Wayne Greenhaw. *The Thunder of Angels: The Montgomery Bus Boycott and the People Who Broke the Back of Jim Crow*. Chicago: Lawrence Hill Books, 2006.

Williams, Timothy. "Sit-in at S. Korean Consulate Protests Hotel's Labor Policies." *Los Angeles Times*, September 25, 1992. http://articles.latimes.com/1992-09-25 /local/me-902_1_south-korean-consulate.

Wilton, Robert D., and Cynthia Cranford. "Toward an Understanding of the Spatiality of Social Movements." *Social Problems* 49, no. 3 (2002): 374–94.

Wong, Kent, Janna Shadduck-Hernandez, Fabiola Inzunza, Julie Monroe, Victor Narro, and

Abel Valenzuela. *Undocumented and Unafraid: Tam Tran, Cynthia Felix, and the Immigrant Youth Movement.* Los Angeles: UCLA Center for Labor Research and Education, 2012.

Wong, Kent, and Michael Viola. *Miguel Contreras: Legacy of a Labor Leader.* Los Angeles: UCLA Institute for Research on Labor and Employment, 2009.

Yinger, Winthrop. *Cesar Chavez: The Rhetoric of Nonviolence.* Pompano Beach: Exposition Press of Florida, 1975.

Zinn, Howard. *SNCC: The New Abolitionists.* Boston: Beacon Press, [1964].

CONTRIBUTORS

ALMA MIRELL CASTREJON was born in Mexico City and at the age of seven migrated to the United States. She earned a dual BA in political science and Chicano studies from the University of California, Riverside, and an ME from California State University, Long Beach.

SOPHIA CHENG graduated from UCLA with an MA in Asian American studies. She works as a community organizer at the Restaurant Opportunities Center of Los Angeles, a worker center for restaurant workers and the local affiliate of ROC United.

ANA LUZ GONZÁLEZ received her PhD in urban planning from UCLA in 2015. Her dissertation, "Formalizing Day Labor Markets: Worker Centers and Worker Integration," investigates the efficacy of worker centers in three areas: labor market outcomes, the mitigation of abuse and hazards, and the civic integration of workers into the communities in which they work and live. For over a decade she has worked as a researcher associate and has managed and led local and national projects for the Center for the Study of Urban Poverty, the Labor Center, and the Institute for Research on Labor and Employment at UCLA. Ana Luz is currently the project coordinator of the UC Irvine Community and Labor Project at the UCI School of Law.

MAYRA JONES is an immigration, labor, and women's rights activist. She graduated from UCLA in 2013 with a BA in philosophy and a double minor in labor and workplace studies and Chicana/o studies. She is currently pursuing a career as a community organizer and researcher with hopes to promote social justice and equality and higher education in under-privileged and underrepresented communities.

REV. JAMES M. LAWSON JR. worked as a youth minister in Nagpur, India, where he studied the teachings of Mohandas Gandhi. He was recruited by Martin Luther King Jr. to spread the philosophy of nonviolence and advance the movement to desegregate the South. Rev. Lawson worked as a volunteer staff member for the Southern Christian Leadership Conference and was a founding member of the Student Nonviolent Coordinating Committee. He led the Nashville sit-in campaign, which successfully challenged Jim Crow, and trained a new generation of civil rights activists who organized Freedom Rides and civil disobedience actions throughout the South. Rev. Lawson was also the chair of the strike committee for the Memphis sanitation workers in 1968, which advanced the slogan, I Am A Man, and successfully organized African American public-sector workers. Since moving to Los Angeles in 1974, Rev. Lawson has continued to have a profound impact on peace and social justice movements. He has taught the philosophy of nonviolence to hotel workers, janitors, and home care workers to prepare them for historic organizing victories. He was a founder of the Clergy and Laity United for Economic Justice, and has been at the forefront of campaigns for a living wage. For over a decade, Rev. Lawson has taught a course titled "Nonviolence and Social Movements" in partnership with the UCLA Labor Center.

CAROLINE LUCE is the Ross Postdoctoral Research Fellow at the UCLA Center for Jewish Studies and the lead curator for the Mapping Jewish Los Angeles project. Before receiving her PhD in history from UCLA in 2013, she received fellowships from the New York Public Library, the UCLA Institute for Research on Labor and Employment, the Southern California Historical Society, and YIVO Institute for Jewish Research and served as a teaching fellow for UCLA's General Education Cluster Program. Her dissertation, "Visions of a Jewish Future: The Jewish Bakers Union and Yiddish Culture in East Los Angeles, 1908–1942," explores the complexities of working-class identity and Yiddish-based labor and community organizing in Boyle Heights.

CAITLIN PARKER is a doctoral candidate in US history at UCLA. Her dissertation, "Mayor Bradley's Los Angeles: Urban Governance in Era of Austerity, 1973–1993," examines struggles over economic development during the twenty-year tenure of the city's first African American mayor.

PREETI SHARMA is a doctoral candidate in gender studies at UCLA. Her dissertation, "Raising Eyebrows," explores the racial, class, and gender formations of intimate labor in the beauty service industry in Los Angeles's South Asian threading salons.

KENT WONG is director of the Center for Labor Research and Education at UCLA, where he teaches labor studies and ethnic studies. Previously he worked as staff attorney for the Service Employees International Union in Los Angeles and the Asian Pacific American Legal Center. He has served as the founding president of the Asian Pacific American Labor Alliance and the founding president of the United Association for Labor Education. He is currently a vice president of the California Federation of Teachers. Kent has published numerous books on the US labor movement, popular education, organizing, immigrant workers and students, and global solidarity. One of the highlights of his career has been the opportunity to work and teach with his friend and mentor Rev. James Lawson Jr.